lonely planet
kids

PARIS
City Trails

Helen Greathead

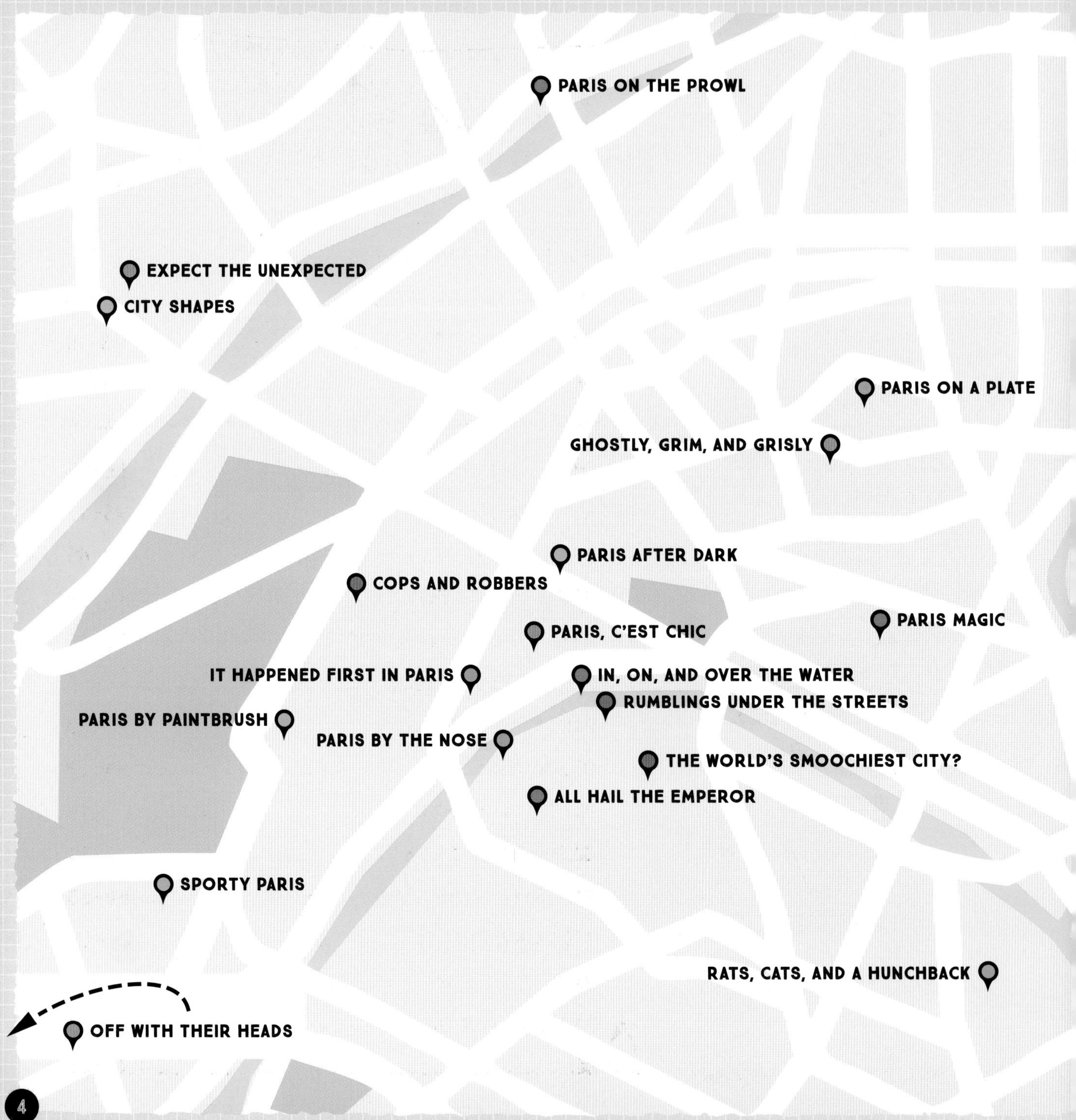

PARIS ON THE PROWL

EXPECT THE UNEXPECTED

CITY SHAPES

PARIS ON A PLATE

GHOSTLY, GRIM, AND GRISLY

PARIS AFTER DARK

COPS AND ROBBERS

PARIS MAGIC

PARIS, C'EST CHIC

IT HAPPENED FIRST IN PARIS

IN, ON, AND OVER THE WATER

RUMBLINGS UNDER THE STREETS

PARIS BY PAINTBRUSH

PARIS BY THE NOSE

THE WORLD'S SMOOCHIEST CITY?

ALL HAIL THE EMPEROR

SPORTY PARIS

RATS, CATS, AND A HUNCHBACK

OFF WITH THEIR HEADS

Hi... we're Amelia and Marco and we've created 19 awesome trails for you to follow.

The pushpins on this map mark the starting points, and each trail is guaranteed to let you in on some of the city's secrets and blow your mind with loads of cool facts. So whether you are a foodie, a sports fanatic, or a movie expert, this book has got something for you!

CONTENTS

EXPECT THE UNEXPECTED

There's much more to Paris than the Eiffel Tower, Arc de Triomphe, and Notre-Dame Cathedral. This is a city that's full of surprises, if you know where to look... it's time to get exploring!

POSH PARIS PARK
PARC MONCEAU

This public park was designed to surprise visitors with its grotto, miniature Egyptian pyramid, and ancient Roman ruins and statues, among other curiosities. The "ancient" exhibits aren't really ancient. They were constructed in 1779 especially for the park – even the graves are fake!

IN OCTOBER 1797, CROWDS IN THE PARK GASPED IN SURPRISE AS DAREDEVIL PARISIAN ANDRÉ-JACQUES GARNERIN MADE THE FIRST-EVER SILK PARACHUTE DESCENT, FROM A HOT AIR BALLOON!

PARC MONCEAU

A BIG THUMBS UP
LE POUCE

Famous French sculptor César Baldaccini had a thing about thumbs. In fact, he liked them so much that he made one that's 39 feet (12 m) tall and cast from 22 tons of bronze! The thumb sculpture erupts from the ground at the center of La Défense, where tourists love to take photos showing their own bitty digits next to this enormous one.

"I feel so small!"

LA DÉFENSE

START

ER... THE STATUE OF LIBERTY?

LADY LIBERTY

IN 1878, THE HUGE HEAD OF THE ACTUAL STATUE OF LIBERTY WAS DISPLAYED AT A WORLD FAIR IN PARIS (THE BODY WAS STILL BEING BUILT). FOR A SMALL FEE, VISITORS COULD CLAMBER AROUND INSIDE THE HEAD.

Isn't that in New York? Well, yes it is. Paris, however, has not just one replica of Lady Liberty, but four! The most famous one stands here at the entrance to the Musée d'Orsay, while a life-sized copy of Lady Liberty's flame guards the road tunnel at Pont de l'Alma. There's good reason for the models, as the original copper statue, weighing 253 tons, was shipped from Paris to New York in 1886 as a gift from France to the US.

MUSÉE D'ORSAY

CINÉMA LA PAGODE

MOVIE PALACE

CINÉMA LA PAGODE

Some say that more movies are shown in Paris than anywhere else in Europe. But not many people have watched a film in an Asian pagoda (temple). This one became a movie theater in the 1930s. It was shipped from Japan in 1895 by wealthy store-owner Monsieur Morin. The pagoda was a gift for Morin's wife, who loved it, but wasn't quite so fond of her husband. She left him a year later!

BEACH LIFE

PARIS PLAGES

With over 100 miles (160 km) to the nearest coast, nobody would visit Paris for its golden sands. However, for a month each summer, the banks of the Seine are transformed into a temporary vacation haven called Paris Plages. Roads are blocked off, sand is imported, and locals and tourists can lounge around in deck chairs, cool off in fountains, lick ice pops at pop-up cafés, play games, and enter sand castle competitions. They can even go surfing, but only on the Internet – the beach has free Wi-Fi!

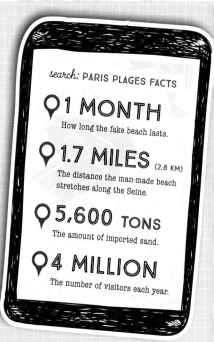

search: PARIS PLAGES FACTS

1 MONTH
How long the fake beach lasts.

1.7 MILES (2.8 KM)
The distance the man-made beach stretches along the Seine.

5,600 TONS
The amount of imported sand.

4 MILLION
The number of visitors each year.

BANKS OF THE RIVER SEINE

MONTMARTRE

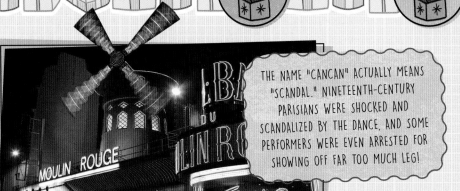

THE NAME "CANCAN" ACTUALLY MEANS "SCANDAL." NINETEENTH-CENTURY PARISIANS WERE SHOCKED AND SCANDALIZED BY THE DANCE, AND SOME PERFORMERS WERE EVEN ARRESTED FOR SHOWING OFF FAR TOO MUCH LEG!

THE WINDMILLS OF OLD PARIS

MOULIN ROUGE

The Paris landscape was once dotted with over 300 windmills (*moulins*). In the past they were essential for grinding wheat and crushing grapes, but only a few remain. The Moulin de la Galette, in Montmartre, is nearly 500 years old and stopped working years ago. Surprisingly, Paris's most famous windmill never worked at all! The sails of the Moulin Rouge (Red Windmill) only turned to draw crowds to the cabaret club beneath it. There, they watched high-kicking girls in swirling skirts dance the cancan.

DO RIDE A DODO

JARDIN DES PLANTES

Considering the dodo died off hundreds of years ago, no one would expect to ride one anywhere in the world... except maybe in Paris! In the corner of the Jardin des Plantes is a very strange carousel. Visitors can whirl around on a dodo, a turtle with horns, a thylacine (aka Tasmanian tiger), a sivatherium (an early ancestor of the giraffe), a panda, or a gorilla. You've guessed, of course, that there's a theme here – these creatures are all extinct or endangered.

MONTMARTRE

THROUGH THE GRAPEVINE

CLOS MONTMARTRE

THE GRAPES ARE PRESSED, FERMENTED, AND BOTTLED IN THE MONTMARTRE TOWN HALL.

Back in the 17th century, the Parisian hills were covered with vineyards, but in the 18th century a deadly disease killed them all off. Today, Clos Montmartre is Paris's only working vineyard, but it hasn't been around for long. In the 1920s, plans to build on this land were halted when a group of local artists came up with a cunning plan. By planting a vineyard, they knew construction could never go ahead. This is because wine is so important in France that it's against the law to build on a vineyard!

16,750 SQ. FT. (1,556 SQ M) OF VINEYARD

1,726 GRAPEVINES

835 PINTS (475 LITERS) OF WINE

950 BOTTLES

ALL SOLD TO FUND COMMUNITY PROJECTS

IN, ON, AND OVER THE WATER

Paris gets its name from the Celtic Parisii tribe, who were attracted to the area in the third century by the huge, rolling river Seine. The watery highway was perfect for ferrying goods and people. Paris has grown up around the Seine, and the river, its boats, banks, and 32 bridges have some surprising stories to tell.

A BRIDGE TOO FAR
PONT ALEXANDRE III

Depending on how you look at it, this bridge is either the most beautiful in Paris, or the most bizarre. It's certainly the fanciest bridge in town – ornate lamps, nymphs, angels, lions, and winged horses and cherubs stand, sit on, or even swing from it. Four pillars at the corners of the bridge thrust golden statues 56 feet (17 m) into the air – the pillars aren't just for show, though, they do in fact help to balance the bridge.

SODDEN STATUE
ZOUAVE DU PONT DE L'ALMA

Hidden beneath the traffic on the Pont de l'Alma, the Zouave statue stands on a platform jutting out over the water. This soldier has been here since the 1850s, when he was installed to celebrate a victory for the Zouave Regiment in the Crimean War. These days, however, he has another purpose: Parisians can tell that the Seine is flooding if its waters lap the statue's boots. Imagine their horror in 2001 when the water reached his knees. Or even worse, in 1910, when the river rose up to his shoulders!

"Please stop honking that horn!"

PONT DE L'ALMA

PONT ALEXANDRE III

START

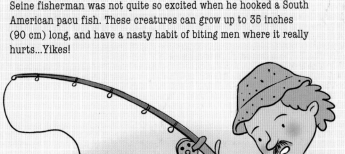

US$16 (€15) IS THE CURRENT FINE FOR JUMPING INTO THE SEINE.

DON'T TAKE A DIP!

THE RIVER SEINE

The banks of the Seine might turn into a beach each summer (see page 8), but Parisians daren't jump into the water – it's illegal! The murky Seine is too dirty to swim in today, but that hasn't always been the case. In the scorching summer of 1716, some bathers were chased off by police – because they were naked! And in a race in 1900, competitors had to swim 656 feet (200 m), climb a pole, and scramble over and under boats. It was the Olympics' first and last watery obstacle race.

A BIT FISHY

THE RIVER SEINE

FISHING IN THE RIVER SEINE

In 2009, locals were excited when 1,000 Atlantic salmon swam through Paris for the first time in over 100 years. In 2013, one Seine fisherman was not quite so excited when he hooked a South American pacu fish. These creatures can grow up to 35 inches (90 cm) long, and have a nasty habit of biting men where it really hurts...Yikes!

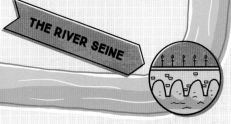

THE RIVER SEINE

THE NEW BRIDGE
– THAT'S 400 YEARS OLD!

PONT NEUF

In the 17th century, Pont Neuf was a design sensation. Its name means "New Bridge," but at over 400 years old, it's now the oldest bridge in Paris! Back in 1607, though, it was thoroughly modern. Who'd ever heard of a bridge with no houses on it? Or one built of stone, not wood... and wider than any city street?

A ROYAL OPENING

In the days when many people paid a boatman to take them from one side of the Seine to the other, the building of a new bridge was a pretty exciting event. And there couldn't be a grander way to open it than for the king, Henry IV, to ride across it on his white stallion.

PUTTING A FOOT DOWN

Horses carried passengers across the bridge in fancy new carriages. Meanwhile, "people of foot" (the word "pedestrian" hadn't been invented yet) had their own part of the bridge to walk on, as Pont Neuf had one of the world's first sidewalks!

PONT NEUF

12 ARCHES
WITH ÎLE DE LA CITÉ
IN THE MIDDLE

| 761 FT. (232 M) LONG | 72 FT. (22 M) WIDE |

BIT OF A JAM

EVERYTHING HAPPENED ON THE BRIDGE: THEATER, MARKET STALLS, FIGHTS, AND SO IT'S NOT SURPRISING THAT IT WAS ALSO THE SCENE OF SOME OF THE WORLD'S EARLIEST TRAFFIC JAMS!

THE BRIDGE WAS A MEETING PLACE FOR RICH AND POOR, BUT IT WAS SAID THAT IF YOU STEPPED ON ONE SIDE WEARING YOUR FANCIEST CLOTHES, YOU'D STEP OFF THE OTHER SIDE WITH NOTHING ON AT ALL!

GETTING AHEAD

No fewer than 381 heads gaze out over the water from the sides of Pont Neuf, and they all have weird and wonderful expressions on their faces. The heads show mythical creatures that are meant to scare off evil spirits.

WRAP IT UP

In 1985, US artists Christo and Jean-Claude used:

450,000 square feet (41,800 sq m) of fabric

8 miles (13 km) of rope

13 tons of steel chains...

to wrap up the bridge!

HENRY IV'S STATUE

WOBBLY CROSSING

WATER AT-TRACTION

You've heard of bounce houses, but a bounce bridge? Surely not! A competition launched in 2012 challenged architects to design a new bridge across the Seine. One firm drew plans for a blow-up trampoline bridge with slides down the sides. Sadly, the winning entry, called Water At-traction, isn't quite as fun, but because it's made with steel cables and springs, it will at least wobble when people walk across it.

THE RIVER SEINE

BRIDGE TO THE PAST

PONT NOTRE-DAME

THE STONE HOUSES ON PONT NOTRE-DAME WERE CONSIDERED QUITE TRENDY IN THEIR DAY. THEY WERE THE VERY FIRST PARIS RESIDENCES TO BE GIVEN THEIR OWN STREET NUMBERS.

Dating back to the time of the Celts, this crossing started out as two wooden footbridges. They were rebuilt by the Romans, burned down by the Vikings, and rebuilt again in the 15th century – with 30 wooden houses on top. In 1499, the weight of the houses caused the bridge to collapse! Next time, it was built of stone, but it caused so many accidents in the river that it, too, had to be replaced. Today's Pont Notre-Dame looks a bit boring – you'd never guess it had such a history!

PONT NOTRE-DAME

A DROP TO DRINK
CANAL SAINT-MARTIN

Beautiful Canal Saint-Martin is a popular place for a Sunday picnic or stroll; there are songs written about it, pictures painted of it, and it's even starred in a few movies. So you wouldn't imagine that the waterway was originally built to help keep Paris clean! As the population of Paris grew in the 19th century, deadly diseases like cholera and dysentery spread. Emperor Napoléon ordered the construction of Canal Saint-Martin in 1802, to bring freshwater into town.

CANAL SAINT-MARTIN

THE EMPEROR PAID FOR THE SUPPLY OF DRINKING WATER BY TAXING THE DRINK PARISIANS LIKED BEST — WINE!

BE SEEN AT THE PISCINE
PISCINE JOSEPHINE BAKER

One place where Parisians can cool off in the heat is Piscine Josephine Baker. It's a swimming pool that's built on a barge in the Seine. It even has a sliding glass roof so the pool can be used whatever the weather.

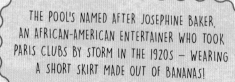

THE POOL'S NAMED AFTER JOSEPHINE BAKER, AN AFRICAN-AMERICAN ENTERTAINER WHO TOOK PARIS CLUBS BY STORM IN THE 1920S — WEARING A SHORT SKIRT MADE OUT OF BANANAS!

PISCINE JOSEPHINE BAKER

PARIS BY THE NOSE

From flowers to freshly baked bread, stinky cheese to even stinkier toilets, many aromas waft around the streets of Paris. While some smells will delight the nostrils, others are downright disgusting!

TOUR EIFFEL

AN EIFFEL OF SMOG
AIR POLLUTION

Traffic congestion is a problem in the city, with air pollution so bad that the Eiffel Tower sometimes disappears completely behind a dirty gray cloud! New rules mean Parisians can now only drive their car into the city every other day of the week. The rest of the time they're encouraged to travel by bike or electric car.

MMM, SMELLY CHEESE PLEASE!
ÉPOISSES DE BOURGOGNE

Fromagerie Alléosse may not sell all of the 400 cheeses France produces, but it does have Époisses de Bourgogne – one of the stinkiest. Époisses is left to mature for several weeks (getting smellier by the day), before it's eaten... with a spoon. In fact, this cheese is so stinky, it's actually banned on public transportation!

FROMAGERIE ALLÉOSSE

GARLIC IS GOOD FOR YOU

PUNGENT GARLIC

Delicious garlicky whiffs waft from cafés and restaurants across the city of Paris. The Romans first brought garlic to France. They believed it was good for their soldiers' courage. In Paris, in 1858, French scientist Louis Pasteur proved that garlic would have protected the men from infection – because it's an antiseptic.

ALL OVER THE CITY

TERRIBLE TOILETS

VESPASIENNE TOILET CUBICLE

The arrival of the "vespasienne" toilet cubicle in 1841 must have been a huge relief – peeing in public had been illegal in Paris since the mid-17th century. The toilet took its name from Ancient Roman Emperor Vespasian, who once taxed the collection of urine from public toilets (people used it to wash their laundry)! The new cubicles were open-sided, made of steel, for men only – they had to stand up – and the smell was.... ugh! Thankfully, boulevard Arago has the very last one.

20,720 TONS OF GARLIC GROWN IN FRANCE EACH YEAR

TO AVOID GARLIC BREATH, EAT AN APPLE OR DRINK GREEN TEA!

BOULEVARD ARAGO

PARISIANS LOVE THEIR POOCHES, BUT THEY DON'T LOVE CLEANING UP AFTER THEM. THE FINE FOR DOG POOP ON THE PAVEMENT IS US$435 (€400), BUT IT'S STILL TOO EASY TO STEP IN THE STINKY STUFF.

EMBARRASSING BODIES

MUSÉE DU PARFUM

In the 15th century, washing went out of fashion – it was thought to be dangerous and unhealthy! New perfumes were developed to cover up the stench. Ingredients were grown in the south of France and sold in Paris, which quickly became the perfume capital of the world. Paris's perfume history is celebrated in Fragonard's Perfume Museum, which has 5,000 years of fragrant tales!

FOUR-LEGGED LAWN MOWERS

JARDIN DES TUILERIES

Freshly cut grass smells a little different when two goats take over from a gas-powered lawn mower. In an experiment at the Tuileries Garden in 2012, the goats did such a great job that now a menagerie of animals are nibbling lawns across Paris in summer. Play "I Spy" two goats in Tuileries, ten sheep at Invalides, and a sheep, goat, and donkey by Paris-Charles de Gaulle Airport!

BREADY FOR BED

BOULANGERIE POILÂNE

The Poilâne bakery dates back to 1932, and it's one of Paris's most famous. Its specialty is a whopping 4-pound (1.8 kg) loaf of sourdough bread, baked in a wood-fired oven. Sourdough lasts much longer than ordinary French bread. In 1971, artist Salvador Dali asked Poilâne to bake him a bedroom out of bread – the chandelier still hangs (unnibbled) in the bakery to this day.

BOULANGERIE POILÂNE

search: PARIS FLOWER FACTS

10,000
The number of sweet-smelling rosebushes in Parc de Bagatelle, one of Paris's botanical gardens.

1808
The year flowers were first sold at the Marché aux Fleurs - Reine Elizabeth II on Île de la Cité.

MAKING SCENTS

BULY 1803

BULY 1803

This is possibly one of Paris's most fragrant shops. It was first opened over 200 years ago by Jean-Vincent Bully, whose signature perfume, Vinaigre de Bully (Bully vinegar!), was a 19th-century sensation. Inside the shop it's like stepping back in time. For a boar-bristle hairbrush, some emu oil, or an actual bottle of the famous scent, look no further. And with no added ingredients, everything in here is nice and natural.

CITY SHAPES

Paris is crammed with stunning historic architecture, but there are also plenty of exciting new buildings and structures popping up around the city, too... come and take a peek!

THE MONUMENT WITH THE HOLE

GRANDE ARCHE DE LA DÉFENSE

In 1989, Grande Arche was built in La Défense (Paris's business district) to celebrate the 200th anniversary of the French Revolution. This huge 361-foot (110 m) cube with a hole in the middle lies on a long straight road that stretches across Paris, past the Arc de Triomphe, all the way to the Louvre. The hole in the middle of the Arche is so huge, Notre-Dame Cathedral could sit inside it!

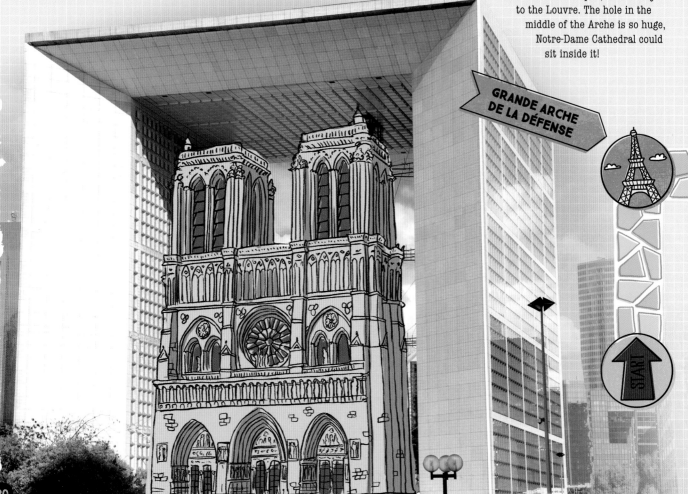

GRANDE ARCHE DE LA DÉFENSE

START

IS IT A SHIP?
IS IT A WHALE?

FONDATION LOUIS VUITTON

No, it's the Fondation Louis Vuitton – a modern art museum. Architect Frank Gehry designed the building, starting with three box shapes for the galleries and three towers for elevators and stairs. Inside, the galleries are simple, but the outside of the building is a work of art. Its 12 curved sails, made from 3,600 panels of glass, are all kinds of shapes.

STAR-STUDDED CITY

PLACE CHARLES DE GAULLE

Place Charles de Gaulle was once known as place de l'Étoile (Star Square) because the 12 roads leading to it make a star shape – with the Arc de Triomphe smack-dab in the middle. In the 1800s, city planner Baron Haussmann was employed by Emperor Napoléon III to clean up Paris's grubby medieval streets. Haussmann introduced drainage, lighting, wider streets, freshwater, and sewers – but threw poor residents out of their homes!

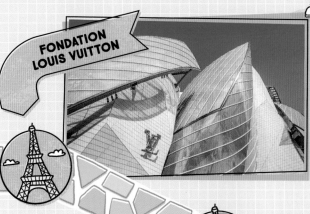

FONDATION LOUIS VUITTON

PLACE CHARLES DE GAULLE

BEFORE HAUSSMANN ARRIVED, PARIS STREETS WERE DARK, DIRTY, AND SMELLED OF POOP! HE TOOK 17 YEARS TO CLEAN UP AND REDESIGN THE CITY.

GOING UP

TOUR TRIANGLE

For years, no one was allowed to build higher than 121 feet (37 m) in central Paris. In 2015, however, plans were approved to allow a 40-story glass tower, shaped like a giant triangle! The architects say the design is to stop too much shadow from falling on nearby buildings. They call the tower "a vertical city."

ARCHITECT'S MODEL

TOUR TRIANGLE

A BIT OF AN EIFFEL

TOUR EIFFEL

Paris's iconic Eiffel Tower was built for the World Fair in 1889, 100 years after the French Revolution. It was erected as a temporary structure, but has towered over the city ever since. The "metal asparagus," as some locals call it, was the tallest structure in the world for 41 years – it's still the tallest in Paris.

THE OBJECT OF OBJECTIONS

Today, the outline of the tower is the most famous shape in the city, but before it was built, many Parisians were furious at the very idea of it. A group of important artists wrote a letter in protest. They called the tower "useless and monstrous" and claimed it would "humiliate" the beautiful buildings of Paris. By 1889, some of them had changed their minds; a composer even wrote a piece of music inspired by the tower.

TOUR EIFFEL

THE ONLY WAY IS UP!

IN 2015 THE EIFFEL TOWER HOSTED ITS FIRST-EVER VERTICAL RACE UP THE 1,665 STEPS. POLISH ATHLETE PIOTR LOBODZINSKI WON, REACHING THE TOP IN AN ASTONISHING 7 MINUTES 50 SECONDS!

search: EIFFEL TOWER FACTS

5 IN. (13 CM)
The distance the tower swayed during a huge storm in 1999.

1,063 FT. (324 M)
The total height of the tower.

5,300
The number of drawings and designs produced by the 50 engineers and designers working on the tower with Gustave Eiffel.

20,000
The number of lights that twinkle on the tower at nighttime, for six minutes every hour, on the hour.

SUPPORTED BY SCIENCE

Scientists were all in favor of the structure. From the start, the tower's designer, Gustave Eiffel, had pointed out its importance to science. He built the tower from iron, because it was more resistant than wood and stone, but not too heavy. He built a laboratory inside, with all kinds of equipment for observing the weather and the stars. When the tower was supposed to come down, in 1909, it was saved because of a newfangled radiotelegraph station installed at the top.

PAINT JOB

Every seven years, a team of 25 painters sets out to repaint the whole structure. The job takes around 18 months, and sometimes involves a complete change of color: from red to yellow to bronze. What next... pink or purple?

"Here we go again!"

INSIDE OUT

CENTRE POMPIDOU

Before it opened in 1977, people thought the Pompidou Center looked more like an oil refinery than an arts center – it had all its pipes on the outside! The colors of the pipes show their different uses: green for liquids, yellow for electricity, blue for air, and red for elevators and escalators. Today, the Pompidou Center welcomes up to 25,000 visitors per day.

NO LADDERS AND BUCKETS ARE NEEDED TO CLEAN ALL THE PYRAMID WINDOWS – EVERY THREE WEEKS THE JOB IS DONE BY A REMOTE-CONTROLLED ROBOT!

THE PARIS PYRAMID

THE LOUVRE

In the 1970s, the Louvre art gallery was such a popular tourist attraction that it couldn't cope with the 4.5 million visitors that passed through its doors each year. Architect I. M. Pei had a solution: dig up the museum courtyard and create a new entrance, covered by a vast pyramid-shaped skylight built from 673 panes of tinted glass! The idea worked, but visitor numbers keep on growing – they could reach 12 million by 2025!

THE LOUVRE

24

PLACE DES VOSGES

STYLISH, BUT SQUARE

PLACE DES VOSGES

A palace once stood on Place des Vosges, and crowds would gather on the grounds to watch bloodthirsty jousting tournaments. After King Henry II got a lance in his brain and died a slow, painful death, his wife had the whole place torn down! Fifty years later, Henry IV built this elegant square of red-brick, blue-roofed houses. This is still one of the poshest squares in Paris today.

BIBLIOTHÈQUE NATIONALE

BOOK BUILDING

BIBLIOTHÈQUE NATIONALE DE FRANCE

Each of the four towers of the French National Library is designed to look like an open book. The "books" are 24 stories high and inside they're light and airy, with seats for up to 3,600 readers and researchers! Nearly 10 million books and records are stored here, from medieval manuscripts to books donated by famous French novelist Victor Hugo.

THE WORLD'S SMOOCHIEST CITY?

Just the thought of Paris makes some people feel romantic, and there are certainly some truly romantic places in the city. But, as they say, the course of true love doesn't always run smooth...

ROMANTIC SPOTS IN PARIS

1) TOUR EIFFEL
2) PALAIS GARNIER
3) THE SEINE RIVER
4) CANAL ST-MARTIN
5) MUSÉE RODIN
6) THE LOUVRE
7) THE *JE T'AIME* WALL
8) CHÂTEAU DE VERSAILLES
9) PONT DES ARTS
10) MUSÉE DE LA VIE ROMANTIQUE

SMOOCHY SCULPTURE

THE KISS SCULPTURE, MUSÉE RODIN

The Kiss is one of sculptor Auguste Rodin's most famous works. It was unveiled in 1901 and immediately people saw it as a beautiful symbol of romantic love. But the lovers are characters from a story, and it turns out that the girl already had a husband – oops! The husband went on to kill the kissing couple, and they were doomed to walk through hell forevermore – yikes!

RODIN DIDN'T THINK MUCH OF "THE KISS" – HE CALLED IT "A HUGE KNICKKNACK"!

MUSÉE RODIN

START

WHO WORE THE PANTS?
MUSÉE DE LA VIE ROMANTIQUE

This romantic house was once much visited by novelist George Sand (real name: Amantine-Lucile-Aurore Dupin) and composer Frédéric Chopin. Fred had fallen for George, despite her shocking habit of wearing pants and smoking cigars! The museum contains a whole room re-created from George's house. In one cabinet, forever together, lie plaster casts of George's arm and Fred's hand.

MUSÉE DE LA VIE ROMANTIQUE

THE JE T'AIME WALL

search: WALL, PARIS, JE T'AIME

131 SQ. FT. (40 SQ M)
The size of the wall.

612 Tiles make up the wall. They're made of enameled lava!

1,000 "I love yous" are written on the wall, in 250 different languages.

THE ROMANTIC WRITING... ON THE WALL
THE *JE T'AIME* (I LOVE YOU) WALL

In a hidden corner of Montmartre, what looks like a huge blackboard is actually a wall of hand painted "I love yous" – and a work of art! Frédéric Baron and Claire Kito (no, they're not a couple) created the wall after Frédéric discovered he found it easier to say "I love you" in a foreign language rather than in his native French.

"I HOPE TO LIVE ALL MY VALENTINE'S DAYS BY YOUR SIDE, EVEN IF THERE'LL NEVER BE ENOUGH TO TELL YOU HOW MUCH I LOVE YOU!"

MAIRIE DE PARIS

MARIE
J'ESPERE VIVRE
TOUTES MES SAINT-
VALENTIN A TES COTES
MEME S'IL N'Y EN
AURA JAMAIS ASSEZ
POUR TE DIRE COMBIEN
JE T'AIME ! F.

SOPPY CITY

VALENTINE'S DAY

Each year on Valentine's Day, the city of Paris invites Parisians to e-mail love messages of 160 characters – the best are displayed on digitized public notice boards all over the city. Some people even post marriage proposals!

ALL OVER THE CITY!

HÔTEL DE VILLE

PONT DES ARTS

KISSING IN THE STREET

THE KISS BY HÔTEL DE VILLE

Romance was in the air when photographer Robert Doisneau was commissioned to photograph kissing couples for *Life* magazine in 1950. In 1986, a photo taken outside Hôtel de Ville (City Hall), Paris, was turned into a poster and became an immediate hit. Most of us look at the picture and think of love, but Doisneau only thought of lawsuits. Several people, who thought they were in the picture, demanded thousands of dollars in royalties!

US$169,000 (€155,000) – THE AMOUNT THAT CO-STAR OF DOISNEAU'S PHOTO, FRANÇOISE BORNET, MADE BY SELLING HER SIGNED COPY OF "THE KISS."

UNLOCKING THE LOVE LOCKS

PONT DES ARTS

What could be more romantic than visiting Paris's Pont des Arts with your true love, clipping a padlock to the bridge, and tossing the key into the Seine river to suggest that your love will last forever? One couple did this in 2008, and eight years later, a million others had followed their lead. After a railing on the bridge collapsed in 2014, workers arrived with bolt cutters, hacked off 700,000 love locks, and replaced the railings with plastic panels.

BRUTAL BUT BEAUTIFUL

MUSÉE DELACROIX

Eugène Delacroix was one of the greatest "romantic" painters, so it's surprising that so many of his works are full of blood, death, and destruction! Romanticism wasn't all about couples getting smoochy. It was more about artists discovering their emotions, and showing them through their work. Delacroix was so important to French art that his little apartment has been turned into a museum of his work.

MUSÉE DELACROIX

140 ROOMS

2 HISTORIC HOUSES

600,000 OBJECTS IN THE **MUSEUM**

MUSÉE CARNAVALET

MAD FOR MADAME K

MUSÉE CARNAVALET

Back in the 17th century, Madame Kernevenoy moved to this house on rue des Francs Bourgeois after her husband was killed in a duel. It was her private residence then, not a museum, but she was never short of visitors. Madame K was such a beauty that courtiers lined up at her door, hoping to win her affections. Since her name was tricky to say, they changed it to "Carnavalet" and the name stuck.

OFF WITH THEIR HEADS

Back in the 18th century, French royalty was having a bit too much fun throwing the country's money away. Meanwhile, ordinary French folk could barely afford to feed themselves. The peasants decided to start a revolution, and it wasn't long before heads began to roll...

700 ROOMS

67 STAIRCASES

2,153 WINDOWS

START

RER Ⓒ Paris ↗

CHÂTEAU DE VERSAILLES

A PALACE TO END ALL PALACES

CHÂTEAU DE VERSAILLES

It's probably the most famous palace in the world, but back in 1682, Versailles, a short train (RER) ride away from Paris, was just a humble hunting lodge. France's King Louis XIV transformed it into a palace, adding new buildings and gardens. Then he moved his government here with 6,000 courtiers! He kept adding extras to the palace, including a Hall of Mirrors, a ballroom 246 feet (76 m) long, and a canal 4,921 feet (1,500 m) long in the garden, with real gondola boats shipped in from Venice!

COMMOTION IN THE CAFE

PALAIS ROYAL

Arcades around the gardens of this beautiful palace were filled with shops and cafés in the 18th century, and they drew big crowds. It was from one of these cafés on July 12, 1789, that journalist Camille Desmoulins stood on a table, waved his pistol around, and encouraged suffering peasants to grab some weapons and fight the rich.

"It's time to fight against poverty."

DURING THE REIGN OF LOUIS XVI, FRANCE NEARLY RAN OUT OF MONEY, AND TERRIBLE HARVESTS LED TO FOOD SHORTAGES. PEOPLE GOT ANGRY AND SOME ROAMED THE STREETS IN ARMED GANGS. RUMORS THAT THE KING WAS SENDING TROOPS TO RESTORE ORDER MADE THE GANGS ANGRIER STILL.

◀ PALAIS ROYAL

THE ANGRY MOB

HÔTEL DES INVALIDES

This home for wounded soldiers was set up by Louis XIV in the 1670s, but in the 1790s the French army kept a secret stash of weapons here. On July 14, 1789, fired up by Desmoulins' speech in the café, an angry mob broke into the hotel and escaped with 32,000 guns! Next stop, the Bastille prison...

HÔTEL DES INVALIDES ▶

THE KING WAS ON DISPLAY AT ALL TIMES. ONE HUNDRED COURTIERS WATCHED HIM WASH AND DRESS IN HIS BEDROOM; HE EVEN HAD A CEREMONY FOR TAKING OFF HIS BOOTS!

LONG LIVE THE REVOLUTION!

PLACE DE LA BASTILLE

July 14, 1789, is probably the most famous date in French history. It was the day ordinary people broke into the Bastille fortress prison and the French Revolution really started...

FEARSOME FORTRESS

The Bastille had actually been built in the 14th century to protect Paris from France's long-term enemy, the English. It became a prison in the 17th century. Prisoners were sent here by order of the king. They went directly to jail. No trial? No chance!

RELEASE THE PRISONERS!

On the morning of July 14, 1789, the mob descended on the Bastille. They were men, women, and children, and they were armed with muskets, swords, and anything else that would work as a weapon. A few Revolutionaries tried to discuss things calmly with the prison guards, but then the mob broke into the prison courtyard and the guards opened fire. One hundred rioters were killed, but the fighting didn't stop until the Bastille guards surrendered. Finally, the prisoners were released... there were only seven of them!

THE HUGE PRISON HELD AN AVERAGE OF 40 PRISONERS A YEAR! THE RIOTERS WEREN'T REALLY INTERESTED IN THE PRISONERS; THEY WANTED THE GUNS AND GUNPOWDER THAT THEY KNEW WERE INSIDE.

PLACE DE LA BASTILLE

4me. ARR!
PLACE DE LA BASTILLE

LATER, AT THE PALACE

Once the Revolutionary soldiers took charge, they sold most of the king's palaces to pay the royalty's bills. In October 1789, the royal court moved from Versailles to the Tuileries Palace. Everyone tried to carry on as usual, but the king was more or less a prisoner.

ONE OF THE FIRST HEADS TO ROLL (SAWN OFF BY THE ANGRY MOB) WAS THAT OF BERNARD-RENÉ JOURDAN, GOVERNOR OF THE BASTILLE.

PLACE DE LA BASTILLE

The name "Bastille" can still be seen on street signs and the metro station, but there's not much to see of the old fortress now. The huge July Column in the middle of place de la Bastille actually remembers a different revolution – which happened in 1803!

THE EIGHT TOWERS OF THE BASTILLE STOOD 100 FT. (30 M) TALL, WITH A MOAT THAT WAS 80 FT. (24 M) WIDE.

BASTILLE DAY

JULY 14 IS A NATIONAL HOLIDAY. IN PARIS, EUROPE'S BIGGEST MILITARY PARADE MARCHES DOWN THE CHAMPS–ÉLYSÉES. FIREHOUSES OPEN FOR A TRADITIONAL FUND-RAISING DANCE AND, AT 11 P.M., THE FIREWORKS FROM THE EIFFEL TOWER ARE TRULY SPECTACULAR.

SANS-CULOTTES

FANCY BREECHES

NO KNEES PLEASE!

SANS-CULOTTES

Wealthy upper-class men wore posh silk breeches called *culottes* that came down to their knees. One group of Revolutionary soldiers wore long pants and called themselves *sans-culottes* (without fancy breeches). Wearing long pants showed that the *sans-culottes* soldiers supported the working people.

ALL OVER THE CITY

PLACE DE LA CONCORDE

HEADS START TO ROLL

PLACE DE LA CONCORDE

King Louis was tried for crimes against the people, found guilty, and executed in 1793. Twelve hundred horsemen accompanied his carriage to place de la Concorde, where the sharp blade of the guillotine whooshed down from its tall wooden frame and sliced off his head. A guard held up the head for the crowd to see, and cheers rang out. There would be no more greedy royalty! Today, this is the largest square in Paris. A tall pink obelisk marks the spot where the guillotine once stood.

search: GUILLOTINE FACTS

1791 The guillotine was introduced as the most painless way to execute anyone, rich or poor!

1793-94 The "Reign of Terror"; the guillotine was kept busy, slicing off a shocking 1,343 heads!

1790s Guillotine toys became popular; children chopped off the heads of dolls and even live rats!

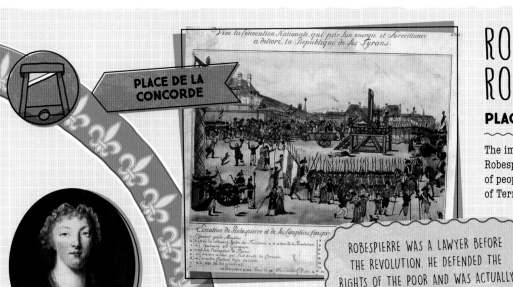

Vive la Convention Nationale qui par son energie et surveillance a delivré la Republique de ses Tyrans.

Execution de Robespierre et de ses Complices Conspi[...]

ROTTEN ROBESPIERRE

PLACE DE LA CONCORDE

The impressively named Maximilien Robespierre condemned thousands of people to death during the "Reign of Terror." He believed that by getting rid of the enemies of the Revolution first, life would improve for everyone later! Funnily enough, his plan didn't work, and in 1794 Robespierre got the chop, too.

PLACE DE LA CONCORDE

ROBESPIERRE WAS A LAWYER BEFORE THE REVOLUTION. HE DEFENDED THE RIGHTS OF THE POOR AND WAS ACTUALLY AGAINST THE DEATH PENALTY!

LA CONCIERGERIE

FIT FOR A QUEEN

LA CONCIERGERIE

Thousands of enemies of the Revolution were thrown in jail during the "Reign of Terror" before being tried and executed. Two thousand prisoners were kept in the huge, medieval palace at the Conciergerie. Many died from the prison's terrible conditions before they even reached the guillotine. The king's wife, Marie Antoinette, was given special treatment – Revolutionary leaders didn't want her to die before they chopped off her head in public!

A LOAD OF OLD BONES

BASILIQUE SAINT-DENIS

For centuries, kings of France were buried at the Basilica of Saint Denis, in the northern suburbs of Paris. However, when Louis XVI and Marie Antoinette were beheaded, they were thrown in a grave with a load of other dead bodies. In 1815, supporters of the monarchs dug up the royal remains and reburied them at the basilica, although rumors say all that was actually buried was a pile of bones and a lady's garter!

BASILIQUE SAINT-DENIS

ALL HAIL THE EMPEROR!

START

While the French Revolution raged, other European countries were threatening France, worried that revolution fever might spread. Napoléon quickly rose through the ranks as he led his country to victory time after time. Take a trail through history to learn how Napoléon soon became France's first emperor.

NOT A CLASS ACT

ÉCOLE-MILITAIRE

Napoléon was born on the island of Corsica in 1769, but he trained at this military school from the age of 15. The school taught him how to use weapons and ride a horse (in later years he taught himself history and geography, and studied the tactics of great kings and generals). He graduated, aged 16, as a second lieutenant, but no one expected much of him – he'd ranked 42nd in a class of 58 students!

10,000
SOLDIERS COULD LINE UP ON THE CHAMP DE MARS
(The field in front of the military school during the 18th century.)

ÉCOLE-MILITAIRE

COMING OUT ON TOP

JARDIN DES TUILERIES

Napoléon proved himself on the battlefield and became brigadier general when he was just 24! After more successful campaigns, he made himself first consul in 1799 – he was more or less in charge of France! Napoléon introduced new laws, which included ideas from the Revolution about freedom and equality. He didn't waste any time before moving into the Tuileries Palace. Only the palace gardens remain today.

JARDIN DES TUILERIES

HAPPILY EVER AFTER?

PLACE VENDÔME

Napoléon fell madly in love with an older woman. Josephine had been married before and had two children, but that didn't matter – Napoléon needed a rich wife. The couple were married in 1796 on place Vendôme. The bronze column in the center of the square was built a few years later. It's cast from recycled cannons captured in battle and celebrates one of Napoléon's glorious victories. He stands proudly on the top – dressed as a Roman.

PLACE VENDÔME

CATHÉDRALE DE NOTRE-DAME

WHO'S THE BOSS?

CATHÉDRALE DE NOTRE-DAME

In 1804, Napoléon decided it was time he was crowned emperor. He reserved Notre-Dame Cathedral and summoned the pope. On the day of the ceremony, to show who was boss, Napoléon arrived late. Then, instead of letting the pope carry out the coronation, he placed the crown on his own head, and then another on Josephine's. The full ceremony lasted over five hours!

190
PEOPLE

featured in the 20x33 ft. (6x10 m) painting Napoléon commissioned for his own coronation. Today it's hanging in the Louvre art gallery.

"I'm keeping my palace!"

DINING OUT
LE GRAND VÉFOUR

LE GRAND VÉFOUR

This classy restaurant has been around for so long that Napoléon and Josephine actually ate here! Napoléon depended on Josephine's intelligence and advice, so they probably discussed tactics at the table. Sadly, Josephine was not quite so fond of Napoléon as he was of her. She complained he had no sense of humor and his boots smelled – but she was as ambitious as he was, and quite liked the idea of being empress of France.

> JOSEPHINE'S FIRST HUSBAND WAS EXECUTED IN 1789. SHE'D HAVE BEEN GIVEN THE CHOP HERSELF IF THERE HADN'T BEEN A CHANGE OF GOVERNMENT JUST BEFORE HER EXECUTION DATE.

DIVORCE AND DEATH
CHÂTEAU DE MALMAISON

When Napoléon realized that Josephine wasn't going to get pregnant, he divorced her to marry someone else. He wanted a son to inherit his expanding empire. Josephine was furious, but there was nothing she could do. Luckily, she'd already bought this fabulous palace, so she had somewhere to live. The palace is still decorated in the style of the 1800s, and Napoléon's rooms are open to the public, as is the fancy bedroom where Josephine died, in 1814.

CHÂTEAU DE MALMAISON

OUSTED

CHÂTEAU DE FONTAINEBLEAU

This was Napoléon's country residence, a long ride away from the city. He redecorated after the Revolution, turning one of the bedrooms into a throne room. His crown and throne are still here today. Josephine's rooms were redecorated when his new wife, Marie-Louise, arrived in 1810. Marie-Louise was Austrian, and a relative of Marie-Antoinette. She only married Napoléon for the sake of her country. Napoléon fled to this comfy castle when the government forced him to give up the empire.

CHÂTEAU DE FONTAINEBLEAU

ARC DE TRIOMPHE

NOT SO TRIUMPHANT

ARC DE TRIOMPHE

Work started on the Arc de Triomphe in 1806, but the arch didn't open until 1836. Unfortunately for Napoléon, France's enemies united against him, and after losing the Battle of Waterloo in 1815, he didn't seem quite so glorious any more. Work on the arch stopped for eight years after Napoléon was exiled to the Island of St. Helena. He died there in 1821. He did, however, travel under the arch in his coffin, when he returned as a national hero in 1840.

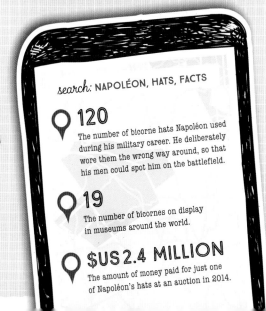

search: NAPOLÉON, HATS, FACTS

120
The number of bicorne hats Napoléon used during his military career. He deliberately wore them the wrong way around, so that his men could spot him on the battlefield.

19
The number of bicornes on display in museums around the world.

$US 2.4 MILLION
The amount of money paid for just one of Napoléon's hats at an auction in 2014.

SPORTY PARIS

Featuring tennis, soccer, basketball, and even France's favorite game of boules, this speedy tour of Paris whooshes past venues for all sorts of sports.

THE RED AND BLUES

PARC DES PRINCES

Allez Paris Saint-Germain is the anthem sung at this stadium, when Paris's top-ranking soccer team plays a home game. The song will be loudest when Paris Saint-Germain (PSG) is playing Olympique Marseille – its biggest rival – and the 45,500-seat stadium is jam-packed.

START

PARC DES PRINCES

STADE ROLAND GARROS

ANYONE FOR TENNIS?

STADE ROLAND GARROS

Tennis originated in medieval France, where monks played it using a cloth ball and their hand. The game spread to the royal courts and became so addictive that it was banned by the church!

Each year in May, 400,000 people flock to Paris's Roland Garros Stadium for the French Open Tennis Tournament. In the unlikely event of a dull tennis match, there's entertainment to be found in the stadium's tennis museum.

RENÉ LACOSTE, NICKNAMED "THE CROCODILE," WAS A TENNIS MEGASTAR IN THE 1920S. HE DESIGNED THE FIRST-EVER TENNIS SHIRTS – WITH A DISTINCTIVE CROCODILE LOGO!

A MONUMENTAL MARATHON

MARATHON DE PARIS

For anyone fit enough, the Paris Marathon is one of the best possible ways to see Paris. The race starts at the Arc de Triomphe and passes the Louvre, Eiffel Tower, and loads more famous monuments on the way to the finish line on avenue Foch.

THE VERY FIRST RACE TOOK PLACE IN 1896, WHEN 200 RUNNERS ENTERED. THEY ONLY GOT A MEDAL IF THEY FINISHED IN UNDER FOUR HOURS!

MARATHON DE PARIS

search: PARIS MARATHON FACTS

26.2 MILES (42.2 KM)
The distance of the race.

50,000
The number of spots available for 2016's event.

140
The number of nationalities likely to take part.

200,000
The number of spectators.

ALL FOR A YELLOW JERSEY!

TOUR DE FRANCE

TOUR DE FRANCE

The Tour de France bicycle race began as a publicity stunt by a journalist trying to increase sales of his magazine. The route changes each year, and can even start in a different country! It normally takes three weeks, covers 3,600 miles (5,633 km), and finishes in Paris on avenue des Champs-Élysées. Winners in different categories wear different-colored jerseys, but yellow is the one to win; it goes to the rider with the shortest total time.

ROLLERMANIA

MONTPARNASSE

At 10 p.m. on a Friday evening, a strange sight can be seen rolling through Montparnasse. Traffic stops as a group of up to 3,500 in-line skaters zip along the wide, smooth streets. The skaters will cover about 19 miles (30 km) in three hours. The roller tour is open to anyone who can keep up with the pack!

> IN FRANCE, CHILDREN AND ADULTS NEED A MEDICAL CERTIFICATE TO COMPETE OFFICIALLY IN ANY SPORT.

MONTPARNASSE

ARÈNES DE LUTÈCE

> IN THE EARLY 1900S, BOULES WERE MADE OF SOLID HARDWOOD COVERED WITH NAILS.

A COOL GAME OF BOULES

ARÈNES DE LUTÈCE

Gladiators once fought for their lives at this ancient Roman arena. Today, its gravel floor is perfect for a cooler, calmer game of boules. All over Paris, small groups of people play the game in flat, shady spaces. First a small wooden ball, or jack, is rolled across the ground, then players take turns tossing their metal "boule" (ball) as near to the jack as they can. The nearest boule wins.

"Keep in line everyone."

ALL OVER THE CITY!

YMCA

RUNNING WILD

PARKOUR

Like Spiderman? Then you'll love parkour. This sport is based on French military training, and was developed in the 1980s by two kids in a Paris suburb. They challenged each other to get from A to B in the shortest distance and time, without letting anything – heights, drops, walls, etc. – get in their way. Thanks to the Internet, the idea really caught on.

"Whoa... don't look down!"

THE PARKOUR CREATORS BECAME FAMOUS IN THE 1990S. THEY'VE BOTH APPEARED IN FILMS – ONE EVEN MADE IT INTO THE JAMES BOND BLOCKBUSTER, *CASINO ROYALE*.

SPORTING HISTORY

YMCA, RUE TRÉVISE

In the basement of a Parisian youth hostel is the oldest basketball court in the world! Basketball was invented in a US college in 1891 – students played with two fruit baskets and a soccer ball! A teacher from the college took baskets and a ball with him when he went to teach in Paris, in 1893, and the YMCA basement was adapted for play. The US college court later burned down, but the Parisian court is still used today (with proper baskets)!

THE PARIS OLYMPICS

OLYMPIC FOUNDER

It was thanks to a Parisian that the first modern Olympics happened in Athens, Greece, in 1896. Baron Pierre de Coubertin loved sports so much that he spent years (and most of his fortune) trying to bring back the ancient games. After he died in 1937, his heart was cut from his body and buried by the ruins of ancient Olympia, in Greece!

3,089
ATHLETES TOOK PART IN THE 1924 OLYMPICS

FROM 44 DIFFERENT COUNTRIES

NOT SO GREAT EVENT

PARIS HOSTED THE SECOND OLYMPICS IN 1900, WITH NO OPENING CEREMONY AND NO LIGHTING OF THE FLAME. WOMEN WERE ALLOWED TO TAKE PART FOR THE FIRST TIME, BUT ONLY 22 TURNED UP – THERE WERE 975 MEN. EVENTS INCLUDED CROQUET, TUG-OF-WAR, ROPE CLIMBING, AND EVEN SHOOTING LIVE PIGEONS. THE FRENCH WON PLENTY OF MEDALS – ALTHOUGH IN SOME EVENTS THEY WERE THE ONLY COMPETITORS!

ERIC LIDDELL WINS GOLD IN THE 1924 400 M RACE

JOHNNY WEISSMULLER

STARS OF SPORT AND SCREEN

In 1924, swimming events drew big crowds, and US swimmer Johnny Weissmuller won three gold medals and a bronze – some still call him the world's greatest swimmer. He went on to star in *Tarzan the Ape Man*. Eric Liddell and Harold Abrahams won 400-meter and 100-meter gold medals respectively for Great Britain, and their story was told in the movie *Chariots of Fire*.

JEUX OLYMPIQUES DE 1924 ARRIVÉE DU 100m ABRAHAMS

HAROLD ABRAHAMS WINS GOLD IN THE 1924 100 M RACE

THE GAMES GET WITH IT

The Paris Olympics of 1924 went so well that we now call them the first "modern" games. The first-ever Olympic Village was built in Paris. It was just a group of wooden huts, but it did have a shop and hairdresser. Athletes were provided with three free meals a day – except for the Brits, who weren't fond of French food so brought their own chef!

THE OLYMPIC MOTTO, "HIGHER, FASTER, STRONGER," WAS USED FOR THE FIRST TIME IN THE 1924 GAMES – EXCEPT IT WAS WRITTEN IN LATIN: "CITIUS, ALTIUS, FORTIUS."

AIMING FOR A CENTURY

Paris has high hopes of winning the bid for the 2024 Olympics, 100 years since the city last staged the games! Opening and closing ceremonies would probably take place in the national stadium, Stade de France, in Saint-Denis.

PARIS ON A PLATE

There's no denying that French people are fond of their food – probably because it's so tasty! How about hot chocolate and a croissant for breakfast, and a chocolate sandwich break at four o'clock? Sounds yummy, but there are a few French foods that might not tickle your fancy quite so much...

€4,000

DAILY BREAD

LE GRENIER À PAIN

It was partly the skyrocketing price of bread that started the French Revolution. Bread is still so important in Paris that every year a contest is held to decide which baker bakes the best baguette (bread stick). In 2015, Djibril Bodian, a baker at Le Grenier à Pain, won US$4,300 (€4,000) and the honor of baking bread for the French president for a whole year.

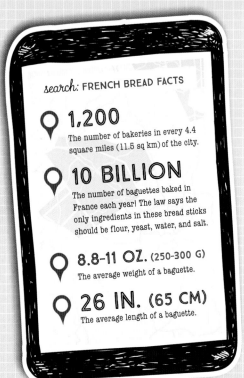

search: **FRENCH BREAD FACTS**

1,200
The number of bakeries in every 4.4 square miles (11.5 sq km) of the city.

10 BILLION
The number of baguettes baked in France each year! The law says the only ingredients in these bread sticks should be flour, yeast, water, and salt.

8.8–11 OZ. (250–300 G)
The average weight of a baguette.

26 IN. (65 CM)
The average length of a baguette.

LE GRENIER À PAIN

START

ROGER LA GRENOUILLE

AGE-OLD DELICACY

ROGER LA GRENOUILLE

The French have been eating frogs' legs (*les cuisses de grenouille*) since the 10th century. Medieval monks weren't allowed meat on certain days of the week, but they persuaded the church that frogs' legs didn't count as meat. Today, French frogs are protected, so the frogs on Paris plates are often shipped in, live, from Asia. Roger La Grenouille bistro has been serving up frogs' legs for over 70 years, cooked Indian or Thai style, with curry or Provençal sauce.

OFFAL SMELL

MOISSONNIER

MOISSONNIER

Andouillette is a French sausage made of cow's stomach lining (tripe). True *andouillette* is oblong in shape, and the sausage skin can be made from colon (innards that store waste food). Some say the tastiest *andouillette* should have a slight smell of poop! *Andouillette* is a popular dish at Moissonnier restaurant, where you can try the famous sausages served boiled or grilled.

FISHY PICTURES

LES HALLES

LES HALLES

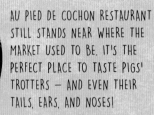

AU PIED DE COCHON RESTAURANT STILL STANDS NEAR WHERE THE MARKET USED TO BE. IT'S THE PERFECT PLACE TO TASTE PIGS' TROTTERS — AND EVEN THEIR TAILS, EARS, AND NOSES!

Novelist Émile Zola called Les Halles "the belly of Paris." Why? Because until 1971, this huge historic market supplied food to the whole of Paris. Vendors sold vegetables during the day, and meat and fish at night.

Greek artist Nonda was a regular nighttime visitor in the 1950s. Being penniless, he painted canvases using cow's blood and charcoal. Nonda would beg vendors for fish, which he painted and then ate!

"I need this fish to hurry up and dry."

THE NICEST ICE CREAM

MAISON BERTHILLON

Tourists flock from far and wide to visit Paris's most famous ice-cream parlor. About 1,760 pints (1,000 liters) of ice cream are made each day from fresh ingredients, including whole milk, eggs, sugar, cream, and natural flavorings such as chestnuts, lavender, and even prunes!

PARISIAN EATERIES

BRASSERIE BOFINGER

Huge trays of seafood, hearty stews, or apple tarts, the traditional food in Paris brasseries looks amazing, and the decor is usually stunning, too. Brasserie Bofinger actually started out as a shabby-looking pub in 1864, but in 1919 it had a complete makeover and reopened – with fancy mirrors, chandeliers, and padded seats – as one of the most beautiful restaurants in Paris.

BRASSERIE BOFINGER

STEAK SURPRISE

AUX DEUX AMIS

The dish to try here is *tartare de cheval*. Finely chopped steak is flavored with onions, capers, anchovies, and parsley, then mixed with mustard and ketchup. It's served with a tiny boiled quail's egg on top. Sound tasty? Did we mention that the meat comes raw – and it's not beef steak? *Cheval* means "horse"!

AUX DEUX AMIS

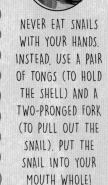

NEVER EAT SNAILS WITH YOUR HANDS. INSTEAD, USE A PAIR OF TONGS (TO HOLD THE SHELL) AND A TWO-PRONGED FORK (TO PULL OUT THE SNAIL). PUT THE SNAIL INTO YOUR MOUTH WHOLE!

ALL OVER THE CITY!

SNAILS FOR BEGINNERS

ESCARGOTS

Snails (*escargots*) are usually served as an appetizer in France. They're stuffed with garlic, parsley, and butter, and then baked. There are only about 300 snail farmers left in France, so 90 percent of restaurant snails are shipped in, frozen, from Eastern Europe. To make sure fresh snails taste tip-top, chefs feed them flour and water for a week, then starve them for three days before cooking.

33,600 TONS

THE WEIGHT OF SNAILS EATEN IN FRANCE EACH YEAR

RUMBLINGS UNDER THE STREETS

A whole different city, filled with underground tunnels, canals, sewers, crypts, and cellars, rumbles under Parisians' feet. Trains trundle along the tracks of the metro for 19 hours a day. It's one of the world's busiest underground railways. Let's go underground and see what we can see.

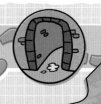

ABBESSES METRO STATION

START

BEAUTY STOP

ABBESSES

At 118 feet (36 m) below ground, Abbesses is the deepest, and also one of the most beautiful, metro stations in Paris. Its entrance is probably the most photographed, too, boasting the fancy art nouveau style that was hip 100 years ago.

SEWER TOUR

MUSÉE DES EGOUTS DE PARIS

MUSÉE DES EGOUTS DE PARIS

Visiting a sewer isn't everyone's idea of fun but, surprisingly, the Paris sewers have been popular since 1867. In those days, the city planners proudly showed off their brilliantly engineered tunnels, and visitors inspected the sewers on special carts suspended over the stinking canals. Today, visits are made on foot, via the sewer museum – and actually, the smell isn't as bad as you might think!

search: PARIS METRO FACTS

📍 **1.5 BILLION**
The number of passengers each year.

📍 **600,000 MILES**
(965,606 KM)
The distance the trains travel each day on the 132 miles (212 km) of track (that's like going around the world 24 times!).

📍 **303**
The number of stations.

METROPOLITAIN

"Hey, where did everyone go?"

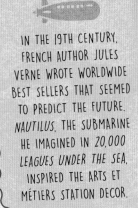

SITTING IN A SUB

ARTS ET MÉTIERS

The platform for line 11 in the Arts et Métiers metro station feels more like it's underwater than underground. With riveted copper walls, portholes, and massive industrial-style wheels in the ceiling, the station gives passengers the feeling that they're inside a science fiction submarine. Which is exactly what the artist intended!

SPOOKY STATIONS

SAINT-MARTIN

The last train stopped at Saint-Martin station years ago and now its tracks have been filled with concrete. The abandoned "ghost" station has been used as a homeless shelter, and also starred in an automobile advertisement.

While it may never see another train, architects' plans show that it could be transformed soon... into a nightclub, an underground garden, or even a long, thin swimming pool!

IN THE 19TH CENTURY, FRENCH AUTHOR JULES VERNE WROTE WORLDWIDE BEST SELLERS THAT SEEMED TO PREDICT THE FUTURE. *NAUTILUS*, THE SUBMARINE HE IMAGINED IN *20,000 LEAGUES UNDER THE SEA*, INSPIRED THE ARTS ET MÉTIERS STATION DECOR.

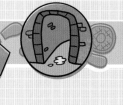

UNDERGROUND TIMELINE
PLACE DU PARVIS NOTRE DAME

As if Notre-Dame Cathedral wasn't ancient enough (construction started in 1163), the square in front of the cathedral hides even more ancient remains. There was a Roman settlement here, and an old stone bath can still be seen, along with signs of underfloor heating! The houses that once crowded the square were knocked down in the 18th century, and the orphanage that replaced them is now just another underground ruin, but together they tell the amazing history of the city.

7,200 SQ. FT.
(2,200 SQ M)
THE AREA THE NOTRE-DAME CRYPT COVERS

It's one of the largest archaeological crypts in Europe.

BAUBLE CROWNS
PALAIS-ROYAL - MUSÉE DU LOUVRE

Welcome to the zaniest station entrance in Paris. Called the Kiosk of the Nightwalkers, it has two giant sparkly crowns hovering over the stairs. Each is made of aluminum poles threaded with 800 colored-glass baubles.

WHAT ABOUT THE HEROINES?

THE PANTHÉON

The Panthéon was built in the 18th century as a church. After the Revolution, it became a resting place for heroes of France, their bodies buried in a spacious crypt underneath the Panthéon. Important people, such as novelists Émile Zola and Victor Hugo, are buried here, alongside great politicians, thinkers, and scientists... all men! A woman was finally honored in 1995, when the ashes of Nobel Prize winners Marie and Pierre Curie were moved here.

THE TOMBS OF GREAT 18TH-CENTURY THINKERS ROUSSEAU AND VOLTAIRE LIE PEACEFULLY OPPOSITE ONE ANOTHER IN THE CRYPT. WHEN THEY WERE ALIVE, THE TWO MEN ABSOLUTELY HATED EACH OTHER.

SECRET STASH

LA TOUR D'ARGENT

La Tour d'Argent (The Silver Tower) restaurant may sit six floors up, but it's the underground cellar that is most famous... for keeping 450,000 bottles of wine and spirits nicely chilled. Some bottles date back to the 18th century!

German forces occupying Paris during WWII forced the restaurant to open for them, but they never found the wine cellar. The owner bricked it up as soon as he heard they were coming!

"Hi Marie, welcome to the crypt."

SKELETONS IN THE BASEMENT

LES CATACOMBES

Sixty-six feet (20 m) below ground, in the limestone tunnels that sprawl beneath Paris, lie the skeletons of 6 to 7 million Parisians. The public can explore 1.43 miles (2 km) of the tunnels, but that's just a fraction of the 186 miles (300 km) that actually exist. Tickets for tomb tours are hard to get hold of, and most of the tunnels are strict no-go zones, but that doesn't stop people sneaking down to take a peek.

A LOAD OF OLD BONES

Skeletons were moved to the catacombs in 1786, when Paris cemeteries became seriously overcrowded. It took two years to transfer the skeletons from just one of the cemeteries – workers brought in piles of bones by wheelbarrow! Famous people and victims of the Revolution are buried here, including some who'd been guillotined, but we'll never know who they were because not one single skeleton has a name attached to it.

THE TEMPERATURE IN THE TUNNELS STAYS A STEADY

57°F (14°C)

ALL YEAR ROUND

THERE ARE THREE TIMES MORE DEAD PARISIANS LYING BENEATH PARIS SIDEWALKS THAN LIVE ONES WALKING AROUND ON THEM TODAY!

ROCK ON

The limestone under Paris has been quarried since the 12th century. The rock was taken to build the city, leaving behind tunnels and some huge underground caves. Major monuments, such as the Notre-Dame Cathedral and the Louvre, were chipped out of this rock.

THERE ARE NO RATS OR BUGS IN THE CATACOMBS, BECAUSE THERE'S NO FLESH ON THOSE BONES FOR THEM TO NIBBLE!

DANGER DOWN BELOW

Set up by the king in 1777, after a series of rockfalls, the General Inspection of the Quarries (IGC) aims to keep the tunnels safe. Today, the IGC is still inspecting, blocking up dangerous parts of the catacombs and sealing off sneaky ways in. But while tunnels have collapsed in the past, and may do so again, the biggest danger is getting lost in the dark!

DODGE THE CATA-COPS!

CATAPHILES – PEOPLE WHO SNEAK INTO THE CATACOMBS.

CATAFLICS – THE POLICE WHOSE JOB IT IS TO KEEP THEM OUT!

UNDER COVER OF DARKNESS, CATAPHILES OPEN UP SECRET ENTRANCES AND CREEP INTO THE CATACOMBS – THROUGH A MANHOLE COVER OR BASEMENT PARKING LOT, PERHAPS. THEY EXPLORE USING MAPS, AND MIGHT HOST A DINNER PARTY! IN 2004, THE CATAFLICS EVEN FOUND A SECRET MOVIE THEATER DOWN THERE!

PARIS, C'EST CHIC

In the 17th century, Louis XIV (the Sun King) wore outrageous big wigs to hide his balding head, and the rest of his court was expected to do the same. That's just one of the ways Paris got into fashion. Today, with the hottest designers and the chicest shops, the city still wears the fashion crown.

HAUTE COUTURE LITERALLY MEANS "HIGH SEWING." IT DESCRIBES THE KIND OF FASHION FOUND ON THE CATWALK — NOT THE ORDINARY STUFF WE WEAR ON THE STREET.

START

PALAIS GALLIERA

HUNG UP ON FASHION

PALAIS GALLIERA

This fashion museum is crammed with clothes from every era, including 200 years' worth of underwear! The museum has 2,500 items in this one department, showing off the changing shapes of bras, bustles (which made rear ends look bigger), corsets, petticoats, stockings, panties, and a whole lot more.

LIBERATED LADIES

FONDATION PIERRE BERGÉ-YVES SAINT LAURENT

In the 1960s, Yves Saint Laurent created "the modern women's wardrobe." He – daringly – dressed women more like men. It's thanks to him that women started wearing jumpsuits, pantsuits, trench coats, and safari jackets. The knitted wedding dress that he designed in 1965 wasn't quite so practical. There are 5,000 Laurent outfits on display here, covering 40 years of fashion history.

FONDATION PIERRE BERGÉ-YVES SAINT LAURENT

LICKING WINDOWS

TRIANGLE D'OR

Three Parisian streets form fashion's Triangle d'Or (Golden Triangle). Inside this area, shoppers can drool over the latest designs from the finest fashion houses. Most people can't afford to buy, but they're not called window-shoppers. In France, the term is *lèche-vitrines* – window lickers!

2,500

People who viewed Dior's new collections in the 1950s. Shows lasted 2.5 hours and showed up to 200 outfits.

WE ALL ADORE DIOR

HOUSE OF DIOR

At 30 avenue Montaigne sits the House of Dior. This is where, in 1947, Christian Dior launched his very first collection. After the rationing and sacklike uniforms of WWII, Dior's dresses were a breath of fresh air. His new designs were "molded to the shape of the female body," showing off the waist, hips, and bust. Dior's new look was called a "revolution in fashion."

THE TRADITIONAL FRENCH SAILOR'S SWEATER HAD 21 STRIPES — ONE FOR EACH OF NAPOLÉON'S VICTORIES. THE DESIGN WAS SUPPOSED TO MAKE SAILORS EASIER TO SPOT WHEN THEY FELL INTO THE WATER!

AN ENGLISHMAN IN PARIS

HOUSE OF WORTH

Living in France in the mid-19th century, Englishman Charles Worth worked his way up from a textile salesman to become dress designer for the French Empress Eugénie. Rich Americans crossed the Atlantic for a whole new wardrobe from the House of Worth. This would often include different dresses to wear in the morning, afternoon, and evening. What lucky ladies!

HOUSE OF WORTH

SKIRTS AND STRIPES

GRAND PALAIS

Jean-Paul Gaultier is one designer who actually grew up in Paris; his first-ever fashion show was at the Grand Palais. Gaultier has always dared to be different, designing skirts for men, and underwear to wear like ordinary clothes. He lists his teddy bear and his grandmother and her corsets as major influences from his childhood, along with stripy sailor tops. Gaultier has designed stripy T-shirts for men, women, and perfume bottles!

FANCY OLD FROCKS

DIDIER LUDOT

What happens to designer dresses when fashion moves on? That's where Didier Ludot steps in, with his collection of vintage designer dresses on display in his famous boutique at the Palais Royal gardens. Didier has a whole line of "Little Black Dresses" (LBDs), like the ones Coco Chanel made popular in the 1920s. Don't ask how much, though. These dresses might be secondhand, but they're still pricey!

€?

€?

LES DOCKS

DIDIER LUDOT

BEFORE THE 1920S, WOMEN ONLY WORE BLACK AFTER SOMEONE HAD DIED. SO THE SIMPLE BLACK DRESS, DESIGNED BY COCO CHANEL TO WEAR ANYTIME, SPARKED A FASHION REVOLUTION.

CROC STYLE

LES DOCKS - CITÉ DE LA MODE ET DU DESIGN

You can call this place "the Docks" for short. Looking like a giant green crocodile, the building stands out from the crowd, just like some of the fashions that parade the catwalk inside. In 2012, the Paris Ethical Fashion Show was held here and featured dresses made from recycled film and old bottle tops!

"Plenty of snappy fashions on show here."

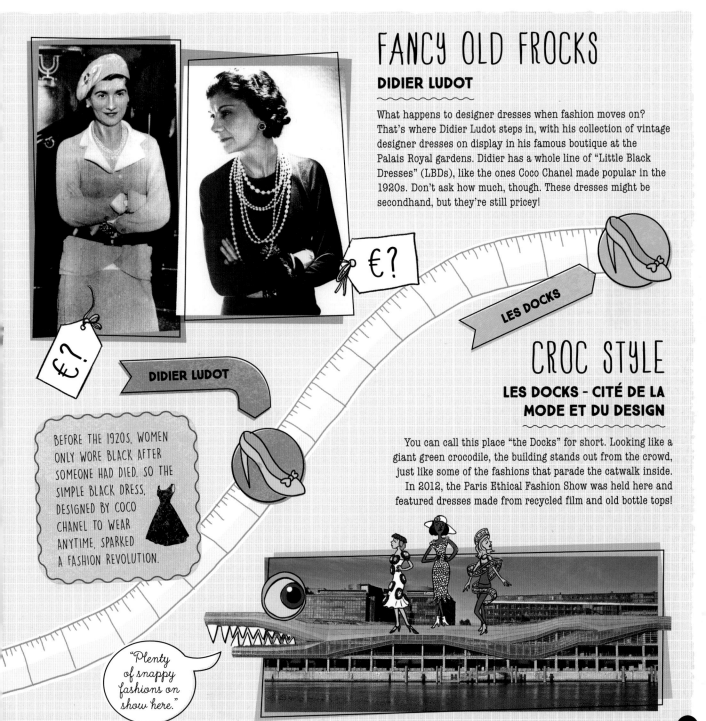

PARIS ON THE PROWL

Even in the heart of the capital, wildlife can pop up in the most unlikely places. Keep your eyes peeled for animals as we take a lively tour around streets, parks, zoos, buildings, and even a cemetery!

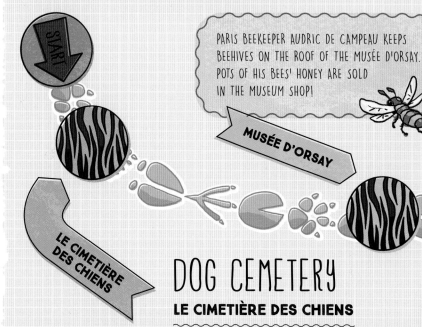

START

PARIS BEEKEEPER AUDRIC DE CAMPEAU KEEPS BEEHIVES ON THE ROOF OF THE MUSÉE D'ORSAY. POTS OF HIS BEES' HONEY ARE SOLD IN THE MUSEUM SHOP!

MUSÉE D'ORSAY

LE CIMETIÈRE DES CHIENS

DOG CEMETERY
LE CIMETIÈRE DES CHIENS

Strictly speaking, Le Cimetière des Chiens is a cemetery for dogs, but other pets – cats, horses, sheep, rabbits, fish, and even a monkey – are buried here, too. Barry the trench dog is the cemetery's biggest hero, though. He's said to have dragged 41 wounded people from a battlefield, and then keeled over from exhaustion!

POMPON'S POLAR BEAR
MUSÉE D'ORSAY

This beautiful polar bear wouldn't look out of place in a Pixar movie, but it's actually nearly 100 years old! François Pompon worked as an assistant to Auguste Rodin – possibly Paris's greatest sculptor – and finally found recognition for his own sculpting skills when this polar bear was unveiled in 1922. By then Pompon was a spritely 67 years old!

GET STUFFED

DEYROLLE

Where would you find a lion, a bear, and a zebra sitting happily side by side? At Deyrolle, of course! Here, the fine art of skinning and stuffing animals (taxidermy) has been practiced since 1831, when big-game hunters brought in their trophy kills to be turned into living room ornaments. The shop and its props have appeared in movies, and artists and writers often stop by for inspiration.

WILDLIFE SURPRISE

RUE DES BLANCS MANTEAUX

There's a lioness on the prowl on rue des Blancs Manteaux. She's a work of art, of course! The photographer who put her there is simply called Sophie. She used to display her pictures in galleries, but says placing them on the walls of buildings, where people least expect them, is much more effective. There's an ostrich down a side street, a penguin on a mailbox, and lots more to spot!

DEYROLLE

RUE DES BLANCS MANTEAUX

CATHÉDRALE DE NOTRE-DAME

CARVED IN STONE

CATHÉDRALE DE NOTRE-DAME

All kinds of scary-looking creatures lurk at the top of Notre-Dame Cathedral. They won't bite, of course, because they're made of stone. People used to think that the creatures came alive at night and swooped around the city protecting the population. Some of these creatures did have another purpose, though – as gargoyles. Pipes in their throats drained the rainwater away from the walls. That way the stonework didn't get damaged.

PARIS GETS A ZOO

MÉNAGERIE DU JARDIN DES PLANTES

In 1793, following the Revolution, it was decided that exotic pets taken from rich citizens and royalty should be brought here to be killed, stuffed, and exhibited for science! The animals did end up in the Jardin des Plantes, but they weren't stuffed – the scientists let them live. The public was allowed in (but not into the enclosures!), and so Paris's first zoo – the second zoo in the world – was created.

BIG-NAME ZOOKEEPER

Jacques-Henri Bernardin de Saint-Pierre (there's a name you won't forget) founded the Ménagerie du Jardin des Plantes in 1794. A strict vegetarian, he was a bit ahead of his time. He believed the zoo animals should live in a natural environment and that the public should be able to see them for free!

IN THE 18TH CENTURY, IT WAS NORMAL FOR ROYALTY TO KEEP EXOTIC PETS. AT THE TIME OF LOUIS XVI, THE PRIVATE VERSAILLES MENAGERIE INCLUDED: A LION, A PANTHER, A TIGER, HYENAS, AND MONKEYS.

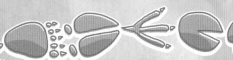

MÉNAGERIE DU JARDIN DES PLANTES

GIRAFFE MANIA

PARIS SAW ITS FIRST GIRAFFE IN THE 1820S, WHEN ZARAFA STROLLED INTO THE CITY. SHE'D WALKED ALL THE WAY FROM HER HOMELAND IN SUDAN AS A PRESENT FOR THE KING. PARISIANS LOVED HER SO MUCH THEY WROTE SONGS AND POEMS ABOUT HER, AND WOMEN INVENTED NEW GIRAFFE-STYLE HAIRDOS! THE FUSS EVENTUALLY DIED DOWN, AND ZARAFA LIVED ON IN THE JARDIN DES PLANTES UNTIL HER DEATH IN 1845.

CHRISTMAS CRAZINESS

In 1870, Paris was surrounded by Prussian troops, and terrible food shortages resulted. Parisians were forced to eat their animals. Not even the zoo animals were spared. Paris chef Alexandre Étienne Choron prepared the most peculiar Christmas meal ever eaten. It included donkey's head stuffed with sardines, fried camel, kangaroo stew, and elephant soup!

STAR ATTRACTION

An orangutan named Nenette arrived at Jardin des Plantes from Borneo in 1972, when she was only two. In 2010, filmmaker Nicolas Philibert was so fascinated by Nenette, and the people who stopped to watch her, that he made a film about her. It's only 15 minutes long, but it took some time to make – Nenette would pose for the camera one day and hide for three hours the next!

NENETTE

search: PARIS ZOO FACTS

32
The number of mammals in the zoo in 1794.

26
The current number of different species of bird.

OVER 3,100 MILES (5,000 KM)
The distance Zarafa the giraffe traveled from Sudan to Paris.

60,000
The number of Parisians who came to visit Zarafa in just three weeks!

RAT-INFESTED RIVER

PARC MONSOURIS

In the peaceful Monsouris park, Parisians can breathe clean air and listen to birds such as kestrels and kingfishers chirping in the trees. The name of the park actually means "mouse hill" – a reference to the rats that once ran around here. The rats were attracted by the river Bièvre, which used to flow nearby. Its waters were so polluted that eventually it was buried under concrete and diverted into the Paris sewers!

PARC MONSOURIS

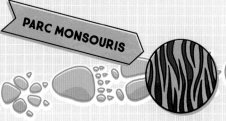

PARC ZOOLOGIQUE DE PARIS

A WHOLE NEW ZOO

PARC ZOOLOGIQUE DE PARIS

When the Paris Zoological Park in Bois de Vincennes reopened in 2014, it was the only zoo in the world to have been completely rebuilt. Animals now exist in five separate zones, which are designed to be as close to their natural habitat as possible. So, giraffes live alongside ostriches and zebras with rhinos – but lions still have an enclosure of their own! For an extra fee, visitors can make a reservation to eat breakfast with the giraffes.

MAD ABOUT ANATOMY

MUSÉE FRAGONARD D'ALFORT

Inside the world's oldest veterinary school is a museum of the work of anatomist Honoré Fragonard, the school's first director. It includes misshapen creatures – a colt with one huge eye, a sheep with ten legs, and a perfectly preserved horse with no skin... yuck!

Fragonard was obsessed with preserving creatures. He even had a secret recipe for pickling them. The school began to suspect he was mad and fired him, but his specimens remain perfectly preserved because of the insect repellent he used in his varnish.

MUSÉE FRAGONARD D'ALFORT

1,000

The number of animals in the Parc Zoologique de Paris.

179

The number of different species, including 42 types of mammal and 74 types of bird.

2.5 MILES (4 KM)

Of walkways snake around the new zoo.

IT HAPPENED FIRST IN PARIS

Toys, vaccines, movies, and more... all kinds of inventions, discoveries, and scientific breakthroughs have happened right here in the City of Light.

MUSÉE PASTEUR

CITÉ DE L'ARCHITECTURE ET DU PATRIMOINE

LOUIS THE GREAT

MUSÉE PASTEUR

French scientist Louis Pasteur is best known for his food-preserving technique (pasteurization), as well as his developments in vaccines, which are still helping to save millions of lives today. The Louis Pasteur Institute, founded by the great man himself, houses his apartment, which is now a museum of his life and work, but serious science research happens here, too.

PASTEURIZATION SAVED THE FRENCH WINE INDUSTRY, BUT LOUIS ALSO HELPED THE FRENCH SILK INDUSTRY BY DISCOVERING WAYS TO DESTROY PARASITES IN SILK WITHOUT RUINING THE FABRIC.

PLASTERED ALL OVER

CITÉ DE L'ARCHITECTURE ET DU PATRIMOINE

Plaster of Paris got its name after the Great Fire of London in 1666. Paris had many wooden buildings at the time, and the French emperor feared a similar blaze. He fireproofed the city by insisting wooden buildings were covered in plaster. Plaster comes from a soft mineral called gypsum, and there was plenty of that in the Parisian hills. Plaster of Paris soon became a boom industry. Today, the museum of architecture displays plaster of Paris models of old buildings, pillars, and doorways.

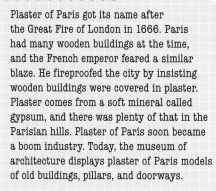

FIRST WOMAN IN SCIENCE

MUSÉE CURIE

The world's most famous female scientist studied in Paris and became the first woman ever to win a Nobel Prize. Among other things, her research into radioactivity made X-rays possible, and she personally took portable X-ray machines to the front during World War I. In the end, Marie Curie's work killed her: she died of exposure to radiation, in 1934.

Marie's old home is now a museum. Her laboratory and office are on display, but you can't see her notebooks. Even after 100 years, they're still too radioactive to read!

PARIS MAGICIAN GEORGES MÉLIÈS MADE OVER 400 SILENT MOVIES. BRINGING HIS MAGIC TRICKS TO THE SCREEN, HE INTRODUCED TECHNIQUES SUCH AS SLOW MOTION AND TIME-LAPSE, AND EVEN CHOPPED OFF LIMBS FOR COMIC EFFECT!

FONDATION JÉRÔME
SEYDOUX-PATHÉ

SILENCE IS GOLDEN

FONDATION JÉRÔME SEYDOUX-PATHÉ

Up until World War I, Charles and Émil Pathé ran the biggest film company in the world! It exists to this day, as Gaumont-Pathé. This brand-new building celebrates Pathé's history, with a whole floor that shows off early cameras, projectors, and other movie machines. A small theater projects old silent movies with live piano accompaniment!

A DROP TO DRINK
PUBLIC DRINKING FOUNTAINS

After the Siege of Paris in 1870, it wasn't just food that was in short supply. The city's aqueducts had been badly damaged, and it was cheaper to drink alcohol than water! Englishman Richard Wallace came to the rescue, paying for over 100 public drinking fountains. The ornate green cast-iron fountains still provide refreshment in the summertime.

IN 2010, A PARIS PARK INTRODUCED CHILLED SPARKLING WATER TO ITS DRINKING FOUNTAINS TO PERSUADE PARISIANS THAT TAP WATER WAS JUST AS GOOD AS THE STUFF IN PLASTIC BOTTLES.

TAXI!
RUE SAINT-MARTIN

Back in 1640, Nicolas Sauvage, a carriage maker, had the bright idea of renting out his horse-drawn carriages by the hour, and so he invented the very first taxi! Twenty years later, a whole system of carriages operated across the city, a bit like bus routes today. Sauvage kept his carriages on rue Saint-Martin, opposite a shrine to Saint Fiacre. Locals called the carriages *fiacres*.

RUE SAINT-MARTIN

KEEP SWINGING

MUSÉE DES ARTS ET MÉTIERS

This is a museum devoted to science and invention; it's full of amazing machines, cars, planes, and all kinds of contraptions. One of its most famous exhibits is a pendulum, the very same one that was used by Léon Foucault in 1851 to prove to Napoléon III that the Earth rotates on its axis each day. The pendulum swung from the museum roof from 1855, until it suddenly smashed to the ground in 2010. Luckily, there's still a working replica in the Panthéon in Paris.

MUSÉE DES ARTS ET MÉTIERS

8,000
THE NUMBER OF OBJECTS IN THE MUSÉE DES ARTS MÉTIERS

4,000
THE NUMBER ON DISPLAY **AT ANY ONE TIME**

ETCH A SKETCH WAS THE FIRST TOY EVER TO BE ADVERTISED ON T.V.

MARCHÉ AUX PUCES DE ST-OUEN

TOY STORY

MARCHÉ AUX PUCES DE ST-OUEN

Turn the two knobs on an Etch A Sketch, and you can draw a picture; shake it, and the picture disappears. Invented in Paris by Andre Cassagnes, it was one of the most popular toys in the world in the 1960s. Etch A Sketch is still being produced today, but Parisians might well find one here, at Europe's largest flea market. It has 2,500 stalls, selling antiques and old toys.

OVER 100 MILLION
ETCH A SKETCH **TOYS SOLD**

PARIS BY PAINTBRUSH

Artists love Paris, and many of them settled here around the end of the 19th century. They were trying out all kinds of daring new techniques... often leaving art critics and the public in shock!

WONDERFUL WATER LILIES

MUSÉE MARMOTTAN MONET

Monet was wild about water lilies in the last 30 years of his life. He grew them in his garden, studied them, and included them in 250 paintings. Early 20th-century critics thought the paintings were messy and blamed Monet's failing eyesight. It wasn't until the 1950s that people really fell in love with them. The Monet museum has the world's largest collection of the artist's paintings and sketches, including a few of his water lilies.

MUSÉE MARMOTTAN MONET

MATISSE DIDN'T EARN MUCH FROM HIS ART AT FIRST. HIS WIFE KEPT THE FAMILY AFLOAT BY WORKING AS A HAT MODEL.

MATISSE, THE BEAST

SALON D'AUTOMNE

In 1905, Henri Matisse shocked visitors to the Salon d'Automne art show with a painting of his wife in a hat. Critics were horrified by his unnatural use of color: a green stripe of paint across her nose, and daubs of yellow, pink, and orange on her cheeks! Matisse and others who painted like this were labeled *les Fauves* (the wild beasts). But Fauvism caught on and became the first art movement of the 20th century.

SALON D'AUTOMNE

€26.8M

ROOM WITH A VIEW

BOULEVARD MONTMARTRE

Camille Pissarro mainly painted countryside scenes, but in the last ten years of his life, he had to stay indoors because of an eye infection. He would set himself up in a top-story Paris hotel room, and paint a bird's-eye view of the streets below. Pissarro didn't have many buyers for his work during his lifetime but, in 2014, his painting *Le Boulevard Montmartre, Matinée de Printemps* (Spring Morning) sold at auction for a cool US$29.8 million (€27.4 million).

MUSÉE RODIN

SCULPTURE SHOCK

MUSÉE RODIN

Auguste Rodin was commissioned to produce a statue of French writer Honoré de Balzac in 1891. He spent six years working on it, missing his deadline by four and a half years! When his patrons saw the model – showing Balzac wrapped in a bathrobe, with huge hair and deep-set eyes – they were horrified! Rodin had focused on the writer's great mind, not the way he looked. The sculptor withdrew the work and never saw it cast in bronze. Today a copy stands in the garden of the Rodin museum.

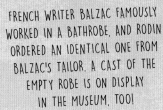

FRENCH WRITER BALZAC FAMOUSLY WORKED IN A BATHROBE, AND RODIN ORDERED AN IDENTICAL ONE FROM BALZAC'S TAILOR. A CAST OF THE EMPTY ROBE IS ON DISPLAY IN THE MUSEUM, TOO!

"Balzac in his bathrobe."

LITTLE DANCER

OPÉRA DE PARIS

Edgar Degas got his inspiration backstage at the Paris Opera House, but in 1881 his sculpture, *Little Dancer*, caused a stir. His model was a poor girl who'd joined the ballet to better herself. He didn't sculpt her from marble, he modeled her from beeswax! And she was wearing a real tutu and ballet shoes, too. People said she looked like an animal. Degas withdrew the sculpture but, after he died, 150 models of the dancer were discovered. Today she's possibly the most famous ballerina in the world.

TOULOUSE-LAUTREC

was just 36 when he died, but he'd produced:

737 CANVASES

275 WATERCOLORS

5,048 DRAWINGS

353 PRINTS AND POSTERS

THE DANCING GIRLS

MOULIN ROUGE

Henri de Toulouse-Lautrec brushed up on his sketching skills in Paris, where he was inspired by a cabaret dancer nicknamed La Goulue (the glutton). He's famous for his posters of the Moulin Rouge, where La Goulue danced, but when she opened a stall at a Paris trade fair, Lautrec painted two huge panels to decorate it. Today those panels hang in the Musée d'Orsay.

MOULIN ROUGE

ESPACE DALI

CHEESY PICTURES

ESPACE DALI

Melting clocks are one of Spanish artist Salvador Dali's trademarks, and there are several examples here at Espace Dali. Dali and the clocks became famous through his 1931 painting *The Persistence of Memory*. Experts speculated that the melting clocks were inspired by Einstein's Theory of Relativity. Dali claimed that they had actually been inspired by Camembert cheese melting in the sun!

MORE THAN A MODEL

MUSÉE DE MONTMARTRE

Suzanne Valadon grew up in Montmartre, working as a waitress, nanny, and circus performer from the tender age of ten. After falling from a trapeze, she began to model for Renoir and others, and gradually learned their skills – Degas even taught her to etch and draw. Her studio was here, in the oldest building in Montmartre, which now houses paintings by artists such as Renoir, Toulouse-Lautrec, and, of course, Valadon.

MUSÉE DE MONTMARTRE

FROM POVERTY TO CELEBRITY

MUSÉE PICASSO

Pablo Picasso (1881–1973) once said, "Give me a museum and I'll fill it." And that's exactly what happened at the Picasso Museum in Paris. It includes works by other artists Picasso liked, but mostly he collected the works of one artist – himself! The exhibits here range from his first paintings, at the age of 14, to his last, at the age of 90.

PAINT SPATTERED

Picasso was Spanish, and he came to Paris at the age of 19, barely able to speak a word of French. He moved to Montmartre in 1904 and lived in a filthy studio, with hardly any furniture and paint spattered everywhere. His girlfriend found a mouse in one of his drawers!

PICASSO'S APARTMENT WAS IN A BUILDING NICKNAMED THE LAUNDRY BOAT, BECAUSE IT CREAKED AND WOBBLED IN THE WIND, LIKE A LAUNDRY BOAT ON THE RIVER SEINE. IT WAS A GREAT MEETING PLACE FOR ARTISTS.

FEELING BLUE

Picasso was poverty-stricken in his first few years in Paris. He couldn't sell his work, and sometimes burned drawings just to keep warm. After a close friend died, Picasso mostly painted miserable works in blue and sometimes visited a local hospital to paint the patients. Things improved, though, and as he started selling paintings, his color scheme changed to pink!

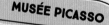

MUSÉE PICASSO

EYES, NOSE, AND A MOUTH

After Picasso and his friend Georges Braque studied African masks in a Paris museum, they began to experiment with their art. Instead of copying what they could see, they showed their subjects in geometric shapes and from different angles at the same time. Picasso said: "A head is a matter of eyes, nose, mouth, which can be distributed in any way you like." This was the beginning of a style of art called cubism.

"THREE MUSICIANS"

NAKED LADIES

LES DEMOISELLES D'AVIGNON WAS PICASSO'S FIRST CUBIST PAINTING, AND MANY PEOPLE THINK IT WAS ALSO HIS GREATEST WORK. IT SHOWED FIVE LADIES... WITH NO CLOTHES ON (YIKES)! IT TOOK PICASSO SIX MONTHS TO COMPLETE, AND WHEN HIS FRIENDS SAW IT, IN 1907, SOME WERE SO SHOCKED BY THE STYLE AND THE SUBJECT MATTER THAT HE DIDN'T DARE SHOW THE PAINTING IN PUBLIC UNTIL 1916.

search: PABLO PICASSO FACTS

1,147
The number of Picassos listed as stolen or missing. His works have the dubious distinction of being stolen more than any other artist's!

90
The number of sittings American writer Gertrude Stein had to make when Picasso painted her portrait.

OVER 5,000
The number of Picassos in the Picasso Museum – and this isn't the only Picasso Museum in Europe!

PAINTING TO THE END

Picasso didn't just paint. He drew, sculpted, made ceramics and prints, and designed stage sets and costumes. He also worked in lots of different styles, changing techniques when he wanted to express something differently. Picasso left Paris a celebrity, but his obsession with his art continued right up until his death, at the age of 91.

COPS AND ROBBERS

French people call their cops "les flics." The flics come in three different varieties. It's the ones with gold buttons on their blue uniforms, hard hats, and guns that get to chase the robbers.

FAKING IT

MUSÉE DE LA CONTREFAÇON

Starting with fake bottle stoppers dating back to 200 BC, the museum of counterfeits has everything from fake toys, perfumes, medicines, car parts, art, and DVDs. They're all placed next to the real thing. Visitors try to guess which are fake and which are real. There's a message behind the museum: fake Barbie goes bald quickly; fake sunglasses don't protect your eyes; and fake medicines... well, let's not even go there!

40 MILLION
FAKE SWISS WATCHES MADE EACH YEAR
That's twice the number that are officially made in Switzerland.

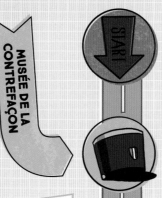

MUSÉE DE LA CONTREFAÇON

START

TRASHED

MUSÉE D'ART MODERNE DE LA VILLE DE PARIS

In May 2010, a brazen thief broke a window and sneaked into the Museum of Modern Art. Three guards missed the intrusion, the alarm system failed to go off, and the thief got away with five priceless paintings that he'd cut from their frames! It was one of the biggest art burglaries ever. A suspect arrested more than a year later claimed he'd panicked when his accomplices were arrested, and thrown the pictures out with the trash!

MUSÉE D'ART MODERN DE LA VILLE DE PARIS

DON'T BAG THAT BARGAIN

EIFFEL TOWER

Tourists might be tempted by look-alike Louis Vuitton handbags or Gucci sunglasses being sold by street vendors near the Eiffel Tower – at a fraction of the cost of the real thing. But this street trade is illegal. When the cops come, the vendors will quickly gather up their wares and run, leaving customers red-handed. Just buying a fake bag is a crime – and the fines cost much more than a real Vuitton handbag.

EIFFEL TOWER

MUSÉE DE LA PRÉFECTURE DE POLICE

COPS AND CRIMES

MUSÉE DE LA PRÉFECTURE DE POLICE

There are 2,000 exhibits in this unusual police museum, some dating as far back as 1667. They include: a bomb hidden inside a flower; a model guillotine (complete with chopped-off head!), and the death masks made of prisoners from centuries ago. Today, the masks can be used to re-create those historic criminal faces and find out how nasty they really looked. Creepy!

OFF THE WALL

PLACE MARCEL AYMÉ

Popular French author Marcel Aymé wrote a short story about an ordinary man who discovers he can walk through walls. The character becomes a thief and uses chalk to write his nickname, Garou-Garou, at the scene of his crimes. The book was a huge hit in France, was made into a film in 1951, and is commemorated in Montmartre. Turn onto place Marcel Aymé, and you'll see a sculpture of the author – walking through a wall!

PLACE MARCEL AYMÉ

THE LOUVRE

MOVING PICTURES

THE LOUVRE

Leonardo Da Vinci's *Mona Lisa* might be the world's most famous painting, but in 1911 hardly anyone had heard of it. In August of that year, a workman at the Louvre hid overnight in a closet, slipped the painting from its frame, and left with it under his jacket. A huge international hunt ensued – it took 27 months to recover the painting. The publicity brought lines of people to the Louvre for the first time ever, and made the *Mona Lisa* a household name.

search: MONA LISA FACTS

7 MONTHS
The jail sentence for the *Mona Lisa* thief.

24 HOURS
The time it took for anyone to notice the *Mona Lisa* was missing.

60
The number of detectives on the case.

US$2.2 BILLION (€2 BILLION)
The estimated value of the *Mona Lisa* in 2014.

RUE DE LA REYNIE

"I don't like the look of those ruffians."

THE FIRST FORCE
RUE DE LA REYNIE

This street is named after Gabriel Nicolas de la Reynie, who became Paris's first lieutenant general of police in 1667, founding the first modern police force. He stayed on the job for 30 years, making sure Paris's posher streets weren't troubled by hoodlums from the wrong side of town!

ALL OVER THE CITY

THE FRENCH SHERLOCK HOLMES
DETECTIVE MAIGRET

France's most famous detective is a pipe-smoking character called Maigret, who stars in 75 novels by Georges Simenon. Many of the stories are set in Paris. Maigret may have been based on real-life detective Chief Inspector Marcel Guillaume. The chief inspector loved the Maigret novels but spotted a few mistakes. So, he invited Simenon to find out what police detective work was really like. The two men became firm friends.

GHOSTLY, GRIM, AND GRISLY

Prepare for a scare or two as you take this tour of some of Paris's spookier corners.

GORY STORIES

LE MANOIR DE PARIS

Welcome to Paris's nastiest attraction. It's a walk-through horror show, with live actors who are out to give you goosebumps as you discover some of the city's darker secrets. There's a choice of legend, like the grisly story of Paris's Philibert Aspairt, who disappeared in the Paris catacombs. His skeleton was retrieved 11 years later, identifiable only by a set of keys on his belt.

START

THÉÂTRE DU GRAND-GUIGNOL

HORROR SHOW

THÉÂTRE DU GRAND-GUIGNOL

Forget horror movies! From 1897, the Grand-Guignol in Pigalle gave theater-goers a real live horror show, complete with eye-gouging, limb-chopping, entrail-ripping torture – oh, and a few murders. It was all done with smoke, mirrors, and buckets of fake blood, but some spectators were so convinced by what they saw they ran screaming from the theater. Grand-Guignol closed in 1962; most people had had enough horror during WWII.

AN EVENING OF
GRAND GUIGNOL
THEATRE OF TERROR

GRAND-GUIGNOL ACTUALLY MEANS THE "BIG PUPPET SHOW"!

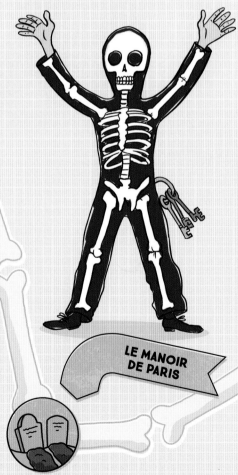

LE MANOIR DE PARIS

THE PHANTOM OF THE OPERA

PALAIS GARNIER

The fabulous, glittering Palais Garnier is the setting for *The Phantom of the Opera*, a novel by Gaston Leroux. The story tells of a ghostly man living beneath the Opera House. It's not hard to see why the author was inspired:

- ➡ The old opera house was destroyed in 1873 by a fire that burned for 24 hours.

- ➡ Built in its place, the Palais Garnier became the biggest opera house in the world. It's riddled with hidden staircases, echoing corridors, and spooky statues.

- ➡ There is a lake deep down in the building's foundations, complete with fish!

- ➡ In 1896, someone died when a chandelier crashed to the ground.

- ➡ Murky underground passageways may connect to other basements nearby.

- ➡ Gaston Leroux swore on his deathbed that the ghost from his story really existed!

PALAIS GARNIER

CIMETIÈRE DES INNOCENTS

INVASION OF THE BODY-SNATCHERS

CIMETIÈRE DES INNOCENTS

In the 16th century, it wasn't ghosts you'd find lurking in this cemetery at midnight, it was doctors and medical students! They were there to snatch the heads, arms, and legs of the dead to help them with medical studies. It was a big risk — the punishment for this crime was a year in prison. One snatcher, Andreas Vesalius, used the knowledge he gained from the graveyard to write a groundbreaking book about the human body.

IN 1780, THE CEMETERY WAS CLOSED — IT WAS OFFICIALLY FULL! BODIES WERE TRANSFERRED TO THE CATACOMBS, AND ANY FLESH THAT HAD NOT FULLY DECOMPOSED WAS RECYCLED INTO CANDLES AND SOAP!

DISAPPEARING BABIES
ORPHAN'S HOSPITAL

Unwanted babies only had a fifty-fifty chance of survival in the 17th century. That's why a priest called Vincent de Paul opened an orphan's hospital here, in 1638. His charity developed a simple system. Moms could put their babies in a box on the side of the hospital, turn a wheel, and, hey presto, the tiny bundles were whisked inside to safety. Mom could then hurry away, no questions asked!

THE BLACK DEATH
HÔTEL-DIEU

First a headache, then a chill, fever, vomiting, and aching limbs; next, lumps started to appear, and oozing black boils and pimples spread all over the body. There was no cure for the Black Death. No one knew what caused it, and the disease spread like wildfire. Nuns cared for the infected here at the city's first hospital, but every day cartloads of dead bodies from the hotel were thrown into a mass grave in the nearby cemetery.

HÔTEL-DIEU

800 — THE ESTIMATED NUMBER OF PARISIANS DYING EACH DAY OF THE BLACK DEATH. IN 1348, HALF OF THE POPULATION OF PARIS WAS WIPED OUT!

BABY IN A BOTTLE
MUSÉE DUPUYTREN

Skeletons, wax models of deformed body parts, diseased organs, and even a baby preserved in a jar are just some of the 6,000 exhibits in this creepy museum. It was first opened in 1835, thanks to a medical professor. Many of the conditions on display are no longer a problem in the West today – maybe that's partly because medics were able to study at this museum?

RUE DES MARMOUSETS

MUSÉE DUPUYTREN

"I won't stop howling until you let me in."

A VERY CLOSE SHAVE
RUE DES MARMOUSETS

A bakery on this street once sold the most delicious pies. The secret recipe was only revealed when a dog wouldn't stop howling outside a nearby barber's shop. The dog's owner had gone for a shave; the barber had slit his throat and sent him through a trapdoor to a butcher below. His "fresh meat" had then turned up in a pie – yuck! If you've heard of Sweeney Todd of 19th-century London, this tale might sound familiar. Except these villains lived in 14th-century Paris!

THE CITY OF THE DEAD

CIMETIÈRE DU PÈRE LACHAISE

A cemetery might not strike you as a top tourist spot, but this is actually the most visited cemetery in the world. It's so huge it even has maps at the entrance to help with navigation through the tombstones. The "streets" are lined with trees and tiny buildings with front doors that hide tombs behind them. Actors, composers, painters, writers, singers... all kinds of people are buried here, many of them superstars of their day.

SELLING THE CEMETERY

When Père Lachaise cemetery opened in 1804, no one wanted to be buried here. At first, there were only 13 graves! So, the administrators staged a clever publicity stunt. They brought in the bodies of already dead celebrities – the playwright Molière and legendary lovers, Abelard and Heloise – and reburied them on the new site. The plan worked, and by 1830, the grave count had reached a satisfactory 33,000.

IRISH WRITER AND POET OSCAR WILDE IS BURIED HERE. FANS TRADITIONALLY TOUCHED UP THEIR LIPSTICK, THEN PUCKERED THEIR LIPS AND LEFT A LIP PRINT ON THE COLD STONE TOMB. WHEN THE AUTHORITIES PUT GLASS WALLS AROUND IT, THE FANS BEGAN KISSING THE GLASS INSTEAD!

TOP OF THE TOMBS

The most visited grave belongs to superstar poet and singer-songwriter Jim Morrison, who died mysteriously in a Paris hotel bath at the age of just 27. Fans still visit every day; some leave poems and messages, others graffiti and cigarette butts. Over 40 years later, Jim's death is still a mystery. One theory says the grave is actually empty and the death was just a hoax.

CIMETIÈRE DU PÈRE LACHAISE

GRAVEYARD GHOSTS

THIS CEMETERY IS SAID TO BE ONE OF THE MOST HAUNTED PLACES IN THE WORLD. STAY HERE AFTER DARK, AND YOU MAY SEE STRANGE LIGHTS AND WISPY FIGURES FLITTING AMONG THE GRAVES. A SHADOWY JIM MORRISON HAS BEEN SPIED WANDERING NEAR HIS OWN GRAVE, AND GET TOO CLOSE TO THE GRAVE OF EX—PRIME MINISTER ADOLPHE THIERS AND HIS GHOST MAY TUG AT YOUR CLOTHES... YIKES!

UP AGAINST THE WALL

In 1871, a group known as the Communards clashed with the French government, and 147 of them were executed beside a wall in the graveyard. Of course, that made burial easy. A trench was dug in front of the wall and the bodies dumped into it. The wall became known as the Communards Wall, and demonstrations are held at the spot in May every year.

search: PÈRE LACHAISE CEMETERY FACTS

109 ACRES (44 HECTARES)
The size of the cemetery.

70,000
The number of tombs.

800,000
The number of people actually buried here.

2 MILLION
The number of visitors to the cemetery each year.

PARIS MAGIC

With magic-themed cafés, shops, shows, and one of the best magicians in the world, Paris really is a magic city.

"Hey dad, I'm flying!"

HOUDINI'S HERO

PALAIS ROYAL

With his top hat and tails, Robert Houdin (1805–1871) created the modern magician's uniform. He was renowned for his extraordinary magic skills, which were far too good for the streets where he first performed. Houdin soon started appearing at theaters, such as the Palais Royal. He had trained as a watchmaker, and he built his own incredible magic props. One was an orange tree that grew real oranges before the very eyes of his audience.

START

ALL OVER THE CITY

TRICKS OF THE TRADE

FAIRS AND MARKETS

Magic shows, as we know them today, really started in the middle of the 18th century. Before that, magicians usually performed at fairs and markets around Paris. They wore strange wizard-like robes and looked a bit weird. Old-style magicians liked to hoodwink the audience into believing they had special powers. Really, they were just performing some old tricks. The whole idea of the magic show changed when Robert Houdin came along.

FAMOUS ESCAPOLOGIST HARRY HOUDINI (1874–1926) TOOK HIS NAME FROM ROBERT HOUDIN, AND EVEN WROTE A BOOK ABOUT THE GREAT MAN — HIS HERO.

PALAIS ROYAL

AUBERGE NICOLAS FLAMEL

"I'm going to live forever!"

HOW TO LIVE FOREVER

AUBERGE NICOLAS FLAMEL

Creating the philosopher's stone (which turns metals into gold) and making an elixir of life (you live forever if you drink it) were the two goals every alchemist dreamed of achieving. Nicolas Flamel and his wife supposedly managed both when they lived here in the 14th century, but not everyone believed them. Whatever the truth, Nicolas certainly lives on in literature – he's been appearing in novels since the 19th century, including *Harry Potter and the Sorcerer's Stone*.

"Ok, no need to lose your head."

"I don't feel too good, I want to stand up."

BOULEVARD DES ITALIENS

TALKING HEADS

BOULEVARD DES ITALIENS

Before Georges Méliès became a filmmaker, he was mad about magic. He probably invented more than 30 new magic tricks, which he used on stage and then in his films. In his most famous trick, Méliès put a man's head (without the body) on top of a table, and the head continued to talk! Méliès was inspired by Robert Houdin, and ended up buying his theater, on boulevard des Italiens.

"This isn't funny anymore!"

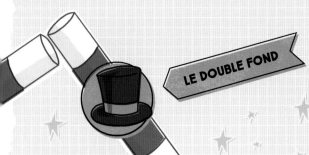

LE DOUBLE FOND

PAST MAGIC

MUSÉE DE CURIOSITÉ ET DE LA MAGIE

History and magic come together in the basement of this little museum. Inside are all kinds of magic props from days gone by — optical illusions, trick cards and gadgets, false-bottomed drawers, and shape-changing mirrors. You can even take a good look at the box that's used to saw a person in half! Some of these items are 200 years old. Special tours are led by magicians, who might also teach a magic trick or two.

MAGIC MEALS

LE DOUBLE FOND

The waiters at this magic café are all magicians, so as well as taking orders, they'll perform a mini-magic show for each table. There's a full magic show downstairs in the basement, and the magicians get so close that guests can really try to figure out the magic tricks. Paris has loads of magic shows and there's even one that floats — on a barge on the Seine.

MUSÉE DE CURIOSITÉ ET DE LA MAGIE

FISHING CAT

RUE DU CHAT QUI PÊCHE

The narrowest street in Paris also has one of the strangest names – Street of the Fishing Cat! It's named after the story of an alchemist's black cat that used to walk down the lane to reach the river Seine, where it always caught a fish. Some students killed the cat, but it's said to have later reappeared and carried on fishing. Spooky, huh?!

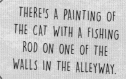

THERE'S A PAINTING OF THE CAT WITH A FISHING ROD ON ONE OF THE WALLS IN THE ALLEYWAY.

MAYETTE MAGIE MODERNE

RUE DU CHAT QUI PÊCHE

SECRETS REVEALED

MAYETTE MAGIE MODERNE

Paris has more magic shops than any other city apart from Las Vegas. Mayette Magie Moderne opened in 1808 and is actually among the oldest in the world! Magicians are usually very secretive about their tricks, but this shop was the first to let ordinary people find out how they work. And if first-time magicians can't get the trick right, they can at least buy all the props here so they look the part.

PICK A CARD, ANY CARD

RATS, CATS, AND A HUNCHBACK

Paris is the setting for many famous French novels, movies, and comic strips. Popular locations around town include museums, shops, and art galleries.

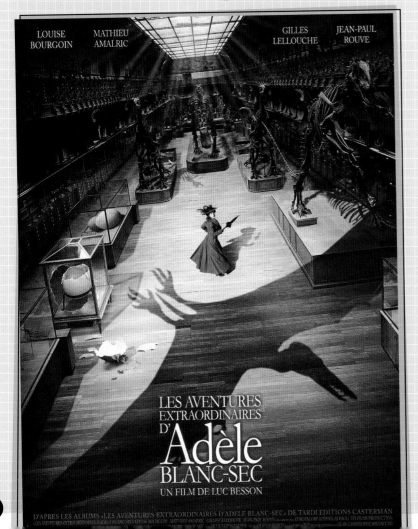

LOUISE BOURGOIN MATHIEU AMALRIC GILLES LELLOUCHE JEAN-PAUL ROUVE

LES AVENTURES EXTRAORDINAIRES D'Adèle BLANC-SEC

UN FILM DE LUC BESSON

D'APRES LES ALBUMS «LES AVENTURES EXTRAORDINAIRES D'ADELE BLANC-SEC» DE TARDI EDITIONS CASTERMAN

MAYHEM IN THE MUSEUM

MUSÉUM NATIONAL D'HISTOIRE NATURELLE

Feisty comic-strip character Adèle Blanc-Sec made it all the way from the corner of a French newspaper, in the 1970s, to a full-length feature film in 2010. Adèle is a no-nonsense kind of girl, who writes for a living, but gets caught up in a lot of mad adventures. The movie starts with a pterodactyl egg hatching in the National Museum of Natural History, then moves on to the pyramids of Ancient Egypt.

ADÈLE'S CREATOR, JACQUES TARDI, KILLED HIS CHARACTER OFF IN 1914, BUT BROUGHT HER BACK TO LIFE IN 1918. HE SAID SHE COULDN'T HAVE COPED IN THE FIRST WORLD WAR, BECAUSE WOMEN WEREN'T ALLOWED TO FIGHT.

HOME FROM HOME

LE CAFÉ DES CHATS

LE CAFÉ DES CHATS

In the Disney movie *The Aristocats*, a butler discovers his rich mistress wants to leave all her money to her cats, so he kidnaps the cats and they have to find their own way back to Paris. The residents of the Cat Café would appreciate the story. They're all strays that have been adopted by the café. Customers can enjoy a drink, a piece of cake, and the company of furry felines.

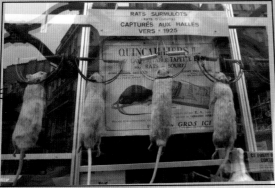

RAT IN THE RESTAURANT

MAISON AUROUZE

Twenty-one dead rats hang in the window of this Victorian pest-control shop, their necks crushed in metal traps. Inside, old shelves and cabinets carry up-to-the-minute poisons and traps. The shop appears in the animated film *Ratatouille*. Lead rat Remy's dad takes him there to show him how humans treat rats. It doesn't stop Remy from going on to become a chef – even though restaurants are some of this shop's biggest customers.

MAISON AUROUZE

CENTRE POMPIDOU

TINTIN IN THE GALLERY

CENTRE POMPIDOU

Hergé, the creator of Tintin, was actually Belgian, but his French-speaking comic-strip hero – and his faithful dog, Snowy – have been popular in Europe for over 70 years. In 2008, a black-and-white strip of Tintin artwork from *The Calculus Affair* was the first comic strip to be accepted as modern art. It's now displayed in the Pompidou Center.

NOTRE-DAME CATHEDRAL

CATHÉDRALE DE NOTRE-DAME

THE HUNCHBACK OF NOTRE-DAME

When Victor Hugo wrote his classic novel about a hunchback called Quasimodo, he never dreamt that more than 100 years later it would be brought to life in films. The 1996 Disney animation, which includes three talking gargoyles, only tells part of the story (the book is nearly 500 pages long!) and has a happy ending. The book does not.

QUASIMODO AND A GARGOYLE, 1939 FILM

DOCUMENTS DISCOVERED IN 1999 SUGGEST HUGO WAS INSPIRED BY A HUNCHBACKED STONEMASON NICKNAMED LE BOSSU (THE HUNCHBACK), WHO WORKED ON THE CATHEDRAL IN THE 1820S.

"Hang on tight."

A NOVEL IDEA

The story takes place around Notre-Dame Cathedral in the Middle Ages. Quasimodo is a hunchback who lives in the bell tower, cut off from the world. His face is disfigured and he's deaf from the ringing of the bells. A gypsy girl called Esmeralda shows him kindness and he falls in love with her. Later, when Esmeralda is sentenced to death, Quasimodo saves her by swinging down on one of the bell ropes and sweeping her to safety.

ON HUGO'S 80TH BIRTHDAY, A STREET IN PARIS WAS NAMED AFTER HIM. TODAY THERE'S A VICTOR HUGO STREET IN JUST ABOUT EVERY TOWN IN FRANCE.

WHO WAS HUGO?

Victor Hugo was born in 1802. He's well known in France, as a poet, playwright, and author of many novels – he wrote 100 lines of poetry and 20 lines of prose every morning! However, it's his two novels, *The Hunchback of Notre-Dame* and *Les Misérables* (also set in Paris), that made him famous abroad. Hugo was one of the first authors to include people from all walks of life in his novels – from kings down to peasants. He gave Charles Dickens a few ideas.

THE BELLS, THE BELLS!

RINGING THE CHANGES

IN 2013, NINE NEW BELLS WERE INSTALLED TO CELEBRATE THE CATHEDRAL'S 850TH BIRTHDAY (THE OLD BELLS SOUNDED AWFUL). EACH NEW BELL HAS A NAME, JUST LIKE THE VERY FIRST ONES, WHICH WERE MELTED DOWN FOR CANNONS DURING THE FRENCH REVOLUTION.

THE REAL HERO

The novel's French title is *Notre-Dame de Paris*, and in fact the cathedral, not the hunchback, was Hugo's real hero. Hugo wanted to make people appreciate Notre-Dame's crumbling Gothic architecture, and he certainly succeeded! The book was published in 1831, and a restoration of the cathedral began in 1844.

COMIC SHOPPING

ALBUM

The French win third place in the world for comic consumption, so Paris has plenty of comic-book shops. One of the best is Album, with two branches – one for French and one for international comics. People are prepared to pay big euros for comic art. At the first-ever comic-strip auction in Paris, 900 enthusiasts turned up. They spent a whopping €3,889,500 (US$4,245,000)!

5,159 COMICS WERE PUBLISHED IN FRANCE IN 2013

DANGEROUS ROBBERY

LES CATACOMBES

Blake and Mortimer are two cartoon characters that are even older than Tintin. First appearing in 1946, this comic-book series was written by a Belgian, but stars two Englishmen – one a scientist, the other from MI5. In *The Necklace Affair*, the two men are at a party when an explosion rocks the building. Blake and Mortimer rush to the cellar, thinking the house has collapsed into the Catacombs below. In fact, Queen Marie-Antoinette's necklace has been stolen – the explosion was caused by a bomb!

LES CATACOMBES

ROMAN AROUND

ARÈNES DE LUTÈCE

In the comic-strip series *Asterix*, Paris is called by its Roman name of Lutetia. France was known as Gaul in those days, and the Romans were in charge. Asterix and his friend Obelix try to resist the Romans with the help of a magic potion that gives them superhuman strength. The amphitheater – the Arènes de Lutèce – is one of the few Roman remains left to see in Paris today.

ARÈNES DE LUTÈCE

search: ASTERIX FACTS

12
films have been made of the *Asterix* books. Eight of them are animations.

107
The number of languages the series is translated into.

5 MILLION
The first print run of *Asterix and the Missing Scroll*, the 36th *Asterix* title, published in 2015.

ASTERIX HAS A FRENCH SPACE SATELLITE NAMED AFTER HIM AND HIS OWN THEME PARK 18 MILES (30 KM) FROM PARIS.

DREAM PARK

DISNEYLAND PARIS

Disneyland Paris isn't actually in Paris, it's a 20-mile (32 km) ride away. Disney wanted the theme park to be further south, where it's warmer, until statistics showed that Paris was easy to reach for 370 million people! The park opened in 1992 and, despite occasional drizzle, by 2015 had welcomed 250 million visitors. Attractions include the stunning Sleeping Beauty Castle and a 4-D Ratatouille experience, with sights, sounds, and smells from the Parisian restaurant featured in the movie.

DISNEYLAND PARIS

PARIS AFTER DARK

Paris got its nickname – the City of Light – because of the philosophers who lived in the city in the 18th century in the "Age of Enlightenment." However, Paris is also a city of lights, and with 300 sights illuminated, it looks amazing after dark.

IN THE SPOTLIGHT
LE GERNY

French singer Edith Piaf was born in Paris in 1915 – according to legend, under a city street lamp. At 14, she performed street acrobatics with her father, but at 15 she switched to singing. When cabaret club owner Louis Leplée heard her singing on avenue des Champs-Élysées, he asked her to sing at Le Gerny. After that first night in the spotlight, Edith's career slowly took off. She went on to become France's most popular singer ever, and the highest-paid star in the world.

START

FESTIVE LIGHTS
CHAMPS-ÉLYSÉES

The Christmas lights are turned on at the beginning of December. Crowds gather to watch the lighting of the 588 trees that line the 1.2 miles (1.9 km) of the avenue des Champs-Élysées. At the end of December, the streets are closed for New Year's Eve, and hundreds of thousands of people gather to welcome the New Year. In 2014, a spectacular video was projected onto the Arc de Triomphe, at the top of the street, in the countdown to midnight.

TINY EDITH WAS ONLY 4 FT. 8 IN. (142 CM) TALL. HER REAL SURNAME WAS GASSION, BUT LEPLÉE CHANGED IT TO PIAF – SLANG FOR "SPARROW."

CHAMPS-ÉLYSÉES

LE GERNY

THE CHAMPS-ÉLYSÉES WAS PART OF BARON HAUSSMANN'S NEW PLAN FOR PARIS IN THE 17TH CENTURY. TODAY IT HOUSES SOME OF PARIS'S POSHEST SHOPS AND CAFÉS.

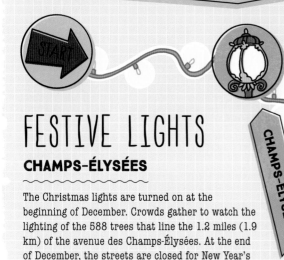

THE TWINKLING TOWER
EIFFEL TOWER

Spectacular light displays have been happening on the Eiffel Tower ever since it opened. The first displays used gas lighting, but the tower turned electric in 1900. From 1925 until 1936, 250,000 colored lamps on the tower spelled out "Citroen" in a giant ad for Citroen cars. In 1937, architect André Granet hung a gigantic chandelier with 6.2 miles (10 km) of colored fluorescent tubes underneath the tower. And, in 1978, 30,000 bulbs turned the tower into a Christmas tree of light.

EIFFEL TOWER

THE BEACON AT THE TOP OF THE TOWER OPERATED AS A KIND OF LIGHTHOUSE FOR AIRCRAFT FROM THE END OF WWII TO 1974.

TOUR MONTPARNASSE

SKY HIGH
TOUR MONTPARNASSE

The fastest elevator in Europe whizzes visitors to the top of the Montparnasse tower. On its 56th floor is a restaurant called Le Ciel de Paris (The Sky of Paris). Up here, customers really feel like they're in the clouds, looking down on the city. The 688-foot (210 m) tower doesn't look too beautiful, but that's okay, because you can't see it from inside. Besides, the nighttime views of the twinkling city are awesome!

"Wow, the lights are amazing!"

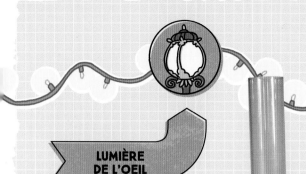

LAMPTASTIC
LUMIÈRE DE L'OEIL

After restoring an oil lamp he found in the street, Monsieur Ara discovered lamps were his passion! He opened his tiny lamp shop in 1976, and he's used some of the more interesting lamps he's collected over the years to create a mini-museum. Now filmmakers come to him for lighting advice, and some of his lamps have made it into international exhibitions.

56,000
THE NUMBER OF GAS STREET LAMPS IN PARIS IN THE 1860s

A LATE 19TH-CENTURY PARAFFIN LAMP

MIDSUMMER MUSIC
FÊTE DE LA MUSIQUE

On June 21, Paris celebrates the longest, lightest day of the year with a fabulous musical party. For one night only, music can be played outdoors in any part of the city. Huge stages appear in public squares, like place de la Bastille, and smaller ones in other squares, gardens, and streets throughout the city. Anyone can take part, so musicians may even perform from a tiny balcony, or an apartment window, for passers-by in the street below.

1,500
CONCERTS
PERFORMED AT THE FÊTE DE LA MUSIQUE
IN 2015

6,000
SPECTATORS
ENJOYED TWO CONCERTS AT THE JARDIN DU PALAIS ROYAL
IN 2015

ALL OVER THE CITY

MARCHÉ AUX PUCES
DE SAINT-OUEN

MOONLIGHTING
MARCHÉ AUX PUCES DE SAINT-OUEN

At the end of the 19th century, junk dealers would scour the streets and trash cans for anything they could sell. Because they worked at night, by the light of the moon, they were called "moon fishermen." The markets those "fishermen" set up to sell their junk became Paris's flea markets, and this is one of the largest in the world!

SLEEPLESS IN PARIS
NUIT BLANCHE

People stay up all night to enjoy the Nuit Blanche (White Night) festival in October. It was inspired by the White Nights festival in St. Petersburg, where summertime brings 24 hours of daylight. In Paris, it does get dark, but art, music, and theater events keep the city awake. During Nuit Blanche in 2014, art group Umbrellium presented their "Mini-Burble" installation at Hôtel de Ville.

INDEX

INDEX